The 5-Ingredient
COLLEGE
COOKBOOK

EASY, HEALTHY RECIPES FOR THE NEXT FOUR YEARS AND BEYOND

Pamela Ellgen

ROCKRIDGE
PRESS

Photography © Stocksy/Trent Lanz, cover; Stocksy/Pixel Stories, cover & p. 56; Stocksy/Davide Illini, p. 2; Stockfood/Jan-Peter Westermann, p. 6; Stocksy/Sara Remington, p. 10; Stockfood/Meike Bergmann, p. 12; p. 24, left to right: Shutterstock/Mayakova & Shutterstock/Maks Narodenko; p. 25, clockwise from top left: Shutterstock/Zcw, Shutterstock/Bigacis & Shutterstock/Andrii Gorulko; Stockfood/Lars Ranek, p. 36; Stockfood/Oliver Brachat, p. 74; Stockfood/Gräfe & Unzer Verlag/Mona Binner Photographie, p. 94; Stockfood/Ian Garlick, p. 110; Stockfood/People Pictures, p. 134; Stockfood/Winfried Heinze, p. 158; Stockfood/PhotoCuisine/Thys/Supperdelux, p. 172; Stocksy/Martí Sans, p. 186; Stocksy/Danil Nevsky, p. 196.

Illustrations © Tom Bingham

Design by Debbie Berne

ISBN: Print 978-1-62315-857-6
eBook: 978-1-62315-858-3

To my parents, for empowering me to go to college.

Contents

5 SOUPS AND STEWS 95

6 VEGETARIAN AND VEGAN MAINS 111

7 SEAFOOD AND POULTRY MAINS 135

8 PORK AND BEEF MAINS 159

9 SWEET TREATS 173

10 KITCHEN STAPLES 187

Introduction

When I moved out of my parents' house and into a college dorm, the only thing I knew how to make with any confidence were chocolate chip cookies. I'm pretty sure I could blend a decent smoothie, scramble some eggs if necessary, and even cook chicken until it wasn't pink in the center. But as far as understanding how to combine ingredients to make food that tasted better than what I could get in the dining hall—how's that for setting the bar low?—I was lost.

Fortunately, I quickly learned that cooking could be both easy and affordable, with immediate (and tasty) rewards. One meal at a time, I gradually built my cooking skills. Whether it was a quick snack or a dinner party entrée, I began cooking for friends, study sessions, and game-day gatherings. My cookies were soon upstaged by Apple Slab Pie (page 183), and friends started to request my Teriyaki Chicken Bowl (page 154). But it didn't happen all at once.

My hope is that through this book you will learn some very basic but incredibly versatile cooking techniques that will serve you well this year and for years to come. The more than 100 recipes in this book are intended to give you confidence and satisfaction in the kitchen. I hope at some point very soon you'll feel empowered to open the refrigerator, see a random assortment of ingredients, and know how to create a healthy, delicious meal with five ingredients or fewer. I want you to feel inspired to walk into a grocery store, glance at what's in season or on sale, and walk out with a dinner plan already formed in your head.

I know that time and money aren't in endless supply in college, but you don't have to sacrifice your schedule, your cash, or flavor to eat well. With only five fresh ingredients and 30 minutes, you absolutely can treat yourself to good-for-you, delicious meals, and build cooking skills to last a lifetime.

Chapter 1

EAT WHAT YOU WANT

The Taste of Freedom

Now that you're the boss of your own menu, you can eat whatever you want. But it's got to be simple, cheap, and fast. And as long as you're cooking, we're going to focus on using fresh ingredients as much as possible (but not too many of them), to keep the unhealthy processed and packaged stuff at a minimum. This chapter is here to help you embrace your newfound culinary freedom by learning what you'll need (and what you won't), plus a few go-to food prep overviews, to take charge of your own kitchen and your meals.

I know that frozen taquitos and the cafeteria cereal bar make compelling arguments for late-night meals. So the recipes in this book are designed to offer an even more convincing appeal. They're easy, inexpensive, and quick. And they taste amazing. Once you start cooking, you'll discover how much better food tastes when you make it yourself.

All the recipes in this book use five main ingredients or fewer, although there are a handful of pantry staples—salt, pepper, oil, red wine vinegar, and spices—that I'm assuming you already have or can easily stock. These pantry staples will be used again and again to ensure you get your money's worth. I also try to use all of each ingredient (in the size it's commonly sold) so you're not left with two-thirds of an onion decaying in your mini fridge.

When you're faced with the proposition of preparing a meal from scratch and cleaning up afterward, or simply opting for takeout, the easiest option will often win. Preparation and cleanup have to be a breeze. That's why all the recipes in this book are designed to go from grocery bag to dinner table in 30 minutes or less, and use a minimal number of dishes—just one pan whenever possible.

As you scan the pages of this book for recipes that might appeal to you, I hope you get excited about having the freedom to cook yummy meals on your own.

Your Kitchen Tools

Some people love gadgets, but I am not one of them. I prefer just a few essential tools that perform a wide variety of tasks. You don't need a lot of fancy utensils to make delicious food. That said, investing in a couple of quality pieces of equipment will save money in the long run and make your cooking experience successful and fun. Here are the tools that I consider essential. You can spend as little as $10 on each piece or more than the cost of a textbook. Ultimately, go for quality, not a name brand, and take care of your tools. You wouldn't leave your shampoo in the dorm shower, and you shouldn't leave your cooking tools in the dorm kitchen.

KNIVES (2). Good-quality knives can last a lifetime—I have had mine for over a decade. A chef's knife and paring knife are essential. A chef's knife is your go-to knife that will be used for slicing, dicing, and mincing. Choose a chef's knife that is about 10 inches long, has a gently curved blade (not serrated), and is sharp right out of the box. A paring knife is great for peeling and ranges in size from 2½ to 4 inches long with a plain blade—that is, a blade that is one continuous sharp edge.

If one is nearby, shop at a culinary store such as Williams-Sonoma or Sur La Table. There, salespeople can guide you to a knife that fits your budget and feels good in your hand. After use, knives should be hand washed and dried. I don't recommend putting them in the dishwasher. Because these knives are sharper than a table knife, be careful to store them safely. It may seem silly but consider wrapping your sharp knives in an old T-shirt or dishcloth before placing them in a drawer. For a quick tutorial on knife skills, see page 31.

SKILLET (1). I recommend a 10- to 12-inch stainless-steel skillet with a heavy bottom, *not* nonstick. Yes, nonstick pans are easier to clean, but they're easily damaged and contain chemicals that may be hazardous to your health. Nonstick pans also don't do a very good job of producing a good sear on meat and seafood. A heavy-bottom skillet will retain and transmit heat better than a thin pan will. It will also reduce your chances of burning foods.

POT WITH A LID (1). Pots are useful for cooking sauces, soups, and stews, and for boiling water for pasta. Choose one with a heavy bottom and a metal or glass lid. I like glass because it allows me to check on the food without letting

steam escape. The heavy bottom distributes heat better and makes scorching food less likely.

RIMMED BAKING SHEET (1). I have written a couple of cookbooks devoted to cooking complete meals on a sheet pan, or baking sheet. I have to say, it's pretty awesome to put your entire meal on one pan, shove it into the oven, set a timer, and have a complete meal with only one dish to clean. I recommend a rimmed baking sheet with a nonstick coating. These pans are useful for roasting vegetables, such as Roasted Squash with Lemon-Garlic Yogurt (page 61), for baking cookies, and for cooking complete meals.

SPATULAS (1 OR 2). A spatula is essential in any kitchen. One silicone spatula should do for all-purpose use. It's great for stirring anything and is especially good for making scrambled eggs, preparing cake batter, and removing all of the food from a container. Personally, I like to have a metal spatula, too. The metal spatula is perfect for sliding underneath seared meat or seafood to make sure you don't leave any of the perfect brown crust on the pan. They're also good for flipping pancakes and hash browns and lifting hot cookies from a baking sheet.

WIDE-MOUTH MASON JARS (4). These jars are great for packing smoothies, soups, and layered salads, and for making chia pudding. While you can buy just one, they're often sold very affordably in packs. Having more than one allows you to be a little lazy with your dishwashing. Make sure you purchase wide-mouth jars, otherwise it can be difficult to get the food in and out. Mason jars tend to come with a ring and a lid, but you'll want to buy a box of additional lids (you can find a pack of 12 lids for under $3). As a bonus, you can also drink tea, coffee, or any beverage in them—they're endlessly versatile. Just keep in mind the glass can get really hot!

Other equipment that is necessary for preparing the recipes in this book includes a colander, whisk, cutting board, glass or ceramic baking dish, measuring cups and spoons, and can opener—things that are likely present in a dorm kitchen, or standard items you'd probably want to have in your apartment kitchen.

Pantry Basics

Pantry staples are the ingredients you should always have on hand because they are used commonly in cooking. They should be shelf stable or keep in the refrigerator for weeks without spoiling. The types and quantities of the ingredients you stock will depend on how often you cook and the kind of cooking you do (e.g., vegan, gluten-free, paleo, low-carb).

The recipes in this book require five ingredients or fewer, but they do assume that you have your kitchen stocked with a few essentials, particularly olive oil and canola oil, sea salt (kosher salt is fine as well), freshly ground pepper, and vinegar. Here are the five essentials you should have on hand all the time. They'll be used frequently in the recipes you'll find in this book and other cookbooks.

Some other helpful ingredients you will want to have on hand are canned plum tomatoes, yellow onions, garlic, dried pasta, rice, and potatoes, but unless you're cooking for yourself every day, you may not want to store them.

COOKING OILS. Extra-virgin olive oil is used when you're dressing salads, cooking vegetables, and making sauces. Purchase a small quantity of extra-virgin olive oil unless you use it often. The oil will last longer if it is kept away from light and heat.

Extra-virgin olive oil is not as heat stable as other oils (such as canola oil and coconut oil), meaning the fats begin to oxidize when heated, and it has a low smoke point of 320°F. This means that extra-virgin olive oil is especially good for salad dressings and other raw preparations where its flavors can shine. That's not to say that cooking with olive oil is bad, but you will lose some of the finer qualities of the oil when you heat it at high temperatures.

Canola oil is used for high-temperature cooking throughout this book. Low in saturated fat and high in unsaturated fats, this oil is widely available, inexpensive, and has little flavor. Store canola oil in a cupboard, and it will keep for four to six months, giving you plenty of time to use the bottle.

SEA SALT. I use fine sea salt in my kitchen because it brings out the flavors in whatever food I'm preparing. Coarse sea salt works well as a finishing salt. Kosher

Brain Food

Staying alert during 8 a.m. classes and focused for marathon study sessions is tough. Add sleep deprivation to the mix, and it can be tempting to reach for easy energy from pastries, chips, and sodas. But these foods don't do your brain any favors. Try these five brain foods instead:

Eggs These are a good source of protein and choline, which are essential for the normal function of all cells, but especially important for the development of your brain and memory function. Try Shakshuka (page 130) for a brain boost.

Nuts These offer a delicious balance of healthy fats, protein, and carbohydrates. Enjoy a handful of nuts as a snack, or make the No-Bake Energy Balls (page 63) for breakfast or as a convenient bite at any time. As a bonus, the caffeine and polyphenols in dark chocolate (which the recipe calls for) can enhance focus and concentration, and improve your mood.

Fish Omega-3 fatty acids, found in abundance in fatty fish such as salmon, herring, and sardines, have been shown to improve cognition and are anti-inflammatory. Choose wild fish whenever possible. Try the Honey-Soy Salmon (page 138) for a delicious dinner.

Avocado This fruit is rich in monounsaturated fat, which improves blood flow and elevates mood. Avocado consumption also increases neural lutein, which improves cognitive function. Try the Tuna-Stuffed Avocado (page 87) and 5-Minute Guacamole (page 188).

Berries The antioxidants in fruits such as blueberries, raspberries, blackberries, and pomegranates help protect your brain from oxidative stress and have been shown to improve learning capacity in clinical trials in rats. Eat fresh berries as a snack or Blueberry Crumble as dessert (page 179).

salt is another suitable option. If you choose table salt instead, use half of the amount called for, and season to taste more cautiously—it's easy to oversalt foods.

FRESHLY GROUND BLACK PEPPER. Technically, you cannot stock your pantry with "freshly ground" black pepper but rather the whole peppercorns and grind them fresh as you need them. Freshly ground black pepper delivers a complex aroma and delicious peppery bite. You may never want to go back to the pre-ground stuff. Don't worry about having to purchase an expensive pepper grinder. Peppercorns are often sold with a grinder in the spice aisle of the grocery store.

RED WINE VINEGAR. Vinegar balances sweet and savory dishes with its acidity. It is essential in making your own salad dressings, which are a cinch with the staples listed earlier. I use red wine vinegar the most, but you may prefer white wine vinegar or apple cider vinegar, which can be used interchangeably when red wine vinegar is called for in recipes in this book. Balsamic vinegar has an assertive, musky, slightly sweet flavor that is delicious but should not be used as a substitute for more neutral-flavored vinegars. Rice vinegar and rice wine vinegar are additional options and are used in Asian cooking.

SPICES. The spices you stock in your pantry depend on the types of food you like to cook. Love Italian food? Choose fennel seed, dried oregano, and crushed red pepper flakes. Prefer Latin flavors? Opt for ground cumin, smoked paprika, and cinnamon. Although you can purchase a spice rack stocked with what someone else decided were the essentials, chances are many spices will go to waste while others are quickly emptied. I prefer to stock my pantry with the spices I know I will use all the time, and wait to purchase others until they're specifically called for in a recipe. For the recipes in this book, you will need the following spices, but not all at once, so buy only if the recipe appeals to you.

cinnamon	curry powder	smoked paprika
chili powder	red pepper flakes	thyme
coriander	rosemary	

Don't Go Broke

Cooking for yourself doesn't have to be expensive. Usually it costs about 25 percent less than eating at a sit-down restaurant. Plus, simple shopping strategies can end up saving you a lot of money. It's important to plan ahead, buy only what you need, choose fresh and inexpensive ingredients, and use up leftovers.

PLAN AHEAD. Plan the number of meals you will make each week. For example, if you have a flexible dining plan at the cafeteria, you might plan to make two dinners and five breakfasts on your own. Then write a list of ingredients those recipes will require. It's nice if there is some overlap between recipes. For example, if you're using 2 tablespoons of minced onion in the Southwestern Skillet (page 51), plan to make Spaghetti Marinara (page 112) for dinner to use the remaining onion. Without a plan, it's easy to spend more money on impulse buys, waste food that doesn't get used before it perishes, and find out that you don't have everything you need when you begin cooking.

BUY FROM THE BULK BINS. Self-serve bins allow you to weigh and purchase just the amount you need. This is a good strategy with dry foods such as nuts, dried fruits, grains, and spices.

SKIP THE FAMILY-SIZE PACKAGING. You know those big-box discount stores that are supposed to save big bucks? Unless you're feeding the entire dorm, you probably won't need that much food, and most of it will go to waste. No savings there!

BUY OFF-LABEL. Sometimes it's worth it to buy the name-brand product, but usually only when the actual ingredients are different from those in the store brand.

SHOP SALES. Grocery stores offer "leader items" at a tremendous discount (sometimes the store even loses money on them). Residents of homes and apartments receive weekly advertisements featuring these sale items, but you can also visit a grocery store's website to download the weekly ad before planning your meals for the week. Or you can sign up for the e-mail mailing list of your favorite grocery store.

LEVERAGE YOUR LEFTOVERS. Many of the recipes in this book include tips on how to use up leftovers in a creative meal the next day. Alternatively, freeze leftovers in individual portion sizes and defrost them later for an instant, healthy meal.

Recovery Food

Whether you spent the weekend partying or at a cross-country meet, chances are your body could use some recovery nutrition. Here are five nutrients you need with foods you can easily prepare that will give your body the fuel it needs to recharge.

Complex Carbohydrates Complex carbohydrates found in sweet potatoes, bananas, brown rice, beans, and quinoa give your brain a steady supply of glucose and replenish glycogen, depleted from your muscles. Insulin is released whenever you consume carbs, and it protects your muscles from catabolism. Just don't go for the simple carbs (white bread, sports drinks, etc.), which set you up for an insulin spike and subsequent low blood sugar. Opt for Sweet Potato Fries with Chipotle Mayo (page 60), or make the vegan BRC Bowl (page 120).

Electrolytes Instead of a sports drink, which is loaded with refined sweeteners and artificial colors, go for a natural recovery drink: coconut water. It is a good source of electrolytes, including potassium, calcium, magnesium, and a small amount of sodium, which help prevent dehydration, reduce fatigue and stress, and improve muscle contraction. Drink coconut water straight, or add some fruit and protein with the Tropical Breakfast Smoothie (page 39).

B Vitamins Drinking alcohol depletes your body of B vitamins. In fact, some of the over-the-counter anti-hangover remedies are little more than a generous dose of B vitamins. You could pop a pill, but enjoying foods rich in B vitamins, such as dark leafy greens, is far tastier. Other good sources of these water-soluble vitamins include asparagus, parsley, broccoli, bell peppers, and lentils. Make the Everyday Kale Salad (page 76) or the Eggplant, Bell Pepper, and Pineapple Curry (page 132).

 Protein Protein is recommended immediately following intense workouts—specifically resistance training—to give muscles the fuel they need to rebuild. Even better is a combination of protein and carbohydrates, which can quickly replenish muscle glycogen and help with protein synthesis. Try the Chicken, Sausage, and White Bean Cassoulet (page 157) or the Teriyaki Chicken Bowl (page 154).

 Probiotics Heavy drinking wreaks havoc on your gut, damaging the population of healthy gut microbes. Foods containing live, active cultures can replenish your gut and strengthen your immune system. Yogurt is the most obvious source of probiotics. Other good sources are fermented foods and beverages, such as kimchi, tempeh, and kombucha. Try the Peanut Butter Yogurt Spread (page 66) or the Loaded Sweet Potatoes (page 125).

The Fresh Stuff

Food prepared with fresh ingredients tastes infinitely better than food made with frozen, canned, and processed ingredients, which often rely on cheap fillers. Bonus: Cooking from fresh is good for your wallet and your waistline.

Here are nine fresh ingredients that show up frequently throughout this book, suggestions on how to buy them, and guidance on how to store them. I buy organic produce whenever I can afford it and when I'm buying foods that typically contain a lot of herbicide or pesticide residue. See the Clean Fifteen (page 200) for more on which fruits and vegetables to buy organic.

1 ONIONS: Many savory recipes in this book include onions. I typically purchase yellow onions, but white onions are fine as well. In raw preparations, I also use red onions. When a recipe uses less than ¼ cup of onion, you can swap it for a shallot, which is smaller in size, so you can purchase just what you need. Choose onions with crisp skins with a slight sheen and no visible signs of mold. Store onions at room temperature.

2 POTATOES: I use fresh russet potatoes in everything from hash browns and oven fries to mashed potatoes and stews. It's fun to experiment with other varieties of potatoes for other recipes; some are more waxy and others are more starchy. Choose firm potatoes that do not have a green tint or any sprouts or moldy spots. Store in a cool, dark place away from onions, which will speed decay.

3 GARLIC: A little goes a long way with garlic, and the fresh stuff is worth the extra effort to peel and mince, especially in raw preparations. Purchase firm heads of garlic with white papery skins and no sign of mold. Many supermarkets also sell jars of preminced raw garlic and roasted garlic. Preminced garlic is fine in cooked dishes, but in raw recipes such as salads and guacamole, fresh garlic is better.

4 TOMATOES: The best tomatoes are bright red or yellow and tender. If a tomato is firm and pale red, it probably tastes bland and mealy. Tomatoes that are still attached to the vine are sometimes better, but not always. Look for a bright color and buy in the summertime and early fall, when tomatoes are in season. In-season tomatoes (and all produce) not only taste amazing, they're less expensive because they're more plentiful. For canned tomatoes, I recommend purchasing whole canned tomatoes and crushing them yourself before use. To do this, simply remove the tomatoes from the can and cut or break apart the pieces before adding them to your dish.

5 HERBS: The recipes in this book sometimes call for fresh parsley, cilantro, basil, thyme, and rosemary. Parsley and cilantro are sold alongside the lettuces. To store them, place the stems in a glass of water and cover them with the plastic bag they were sold in. They will keep for a week or more in the refrigerator this way. You can also store fresh herbs in a plastic bag or puréed in ice-cube trays in the freezer. Rinse and chop them whenever you're ready to use them. Basil, thyme, and rosemary are sold in small plastic packages. Sometimes you can find multiple herb sprigs in one package,

To Wash or Not to Wash?

Before using produce, you should always wash it. The only exceptions are things like onions, garlic, and shallots, which have skin that is peeled off before using.

Most fruits and vegetables can be rinsed under running water to remove dirt and residue. This includes apples, peaches, berries, and other similar stone and seeded fruits.

For lettuce, greens, and other leafy vegetables, submerging them in a bowl or sink of cool water and swish the greens around until dirt is removed. You may have to replace the water a couple of times until it is no longer dirty, depending on the type of greens.

For fruit that will be cut, such as watermelon or cantaloupe, rinse the outer surface before cutting to prevent contamination on the cutting board, which can then transfer to the food.

Although you want to wash fruits and vegetables, what you don't want to wash is meat. Washing meat can splash its juices around your kitchen, and this can contaminate your kitchen and cause foodborne illness. The surface of the meat will be cooked, destroying any bacteria that you would wash off with water in the first place.

which is great when you need only a little bit of each. If you have only the dried herbs, that is fine too. A good rule of thumb when substituting dried for fresh herbs is to use one-third the amount of fresh herb. For example, if a recipe calls for 1 tablespoon of fresh basil, use 1 teaspoon of dried basil instead.

6 **LEMONS**: Fresh lemon juice and zest add brightness, acidity, and flavor that the bottled variety cannot. When you purchase fresh lemons, look for bright, shiny yellow skin without any green. Store them in the refrigerator for the longest shelf life.

7 **AVOCADOS**: Most grocery stores stock unripe avocados because the fruits are so easily bruised. That's okay, though. Simply purchase an avocado a few days before you intend to use it. Avocados are ripe when the skin has a gentle give.

8 **LEAFY GREENS**: Some recipes call for kale and spinach. Choose crisp, not limp, greens, and store them in a plastic bag in the refrigerator. They will keep for one week or more in the vegetable drawer.

9 **BELL PEPPERS**: Red, orange, and yellow bell peppers are sweeter than green bell peppers, which have a more complex flavor. Peppers should be bright in color and firm to the touch.

About the Recipes

I chose the recipes in this book to use just a few inexpensive ingredients that come together quickly and easily and taste amazingly good. The book features new twists on family favorites and some adventurous dishes to bring new flavors to the table. Preparing food should be approachable and fun, and I hope that you find that in every recipe in this book.

Included are labels with each recipe that will help you navigate dietary preferences, including Vegan, Vegetarian, and Gluten-Free. When recipes are especially convenient, I have labeled them as Microwave Friendly, Prep and Serve, and Good for Sharing. Many recipes can be prepared in the microwave more quickly than they can in the oven or on the stove top. Recipes that are labeled "Prep and Serve" require no cooking. Recipes labeled "Good for Sharing" are easily multiplied or have a generous yield for sharing with friends and roommates. I also offer tips on how to make recipes even easier, store and serve leftovers, and improve your culinary knowledge and skills.

Ready to dice, sauté, blanch, purée, and more? If you're new to cooking, maybe not. The meaning of these terms might be unfamiliar, but fear not. A glossary at the end of the book will introduce you to some common terms you're likely to see again and again. Refer to it as often as you need to!

Whether this is your first time cooking or you've been the family chef since you could see over the counter, I hope you find the recipes in this book exciting and original and that they bring the comforts of home to your college experience. I also hope you learn fundamental cooking techniques that empower you in the kitchen, now and throughout your life.

Knife Skills

Having some basic knife skills can help protect your fingers while you are working in the kitchen. It can also ensure that you are able to cut ingredients as recipes instruct, making the whole process of cooking easier.

HOLDING A KNIFE

When you hold the knife in your hand, your thumb should wrap around the base of the blade for stability, while the fingers should wrap around the handle of the knife. The index finger should be directly opposite the thumb, sitting on the opposite side of the blade. Most of your grip takes place with the thumb and index finger, not with the three fingers wrapped around the handle.

GUIDING THE FOOD

Your opposite hand, called the guiding hand, will hold the food on the cutting board to prevent it from slipping around. Because the blade of the knife is so close to your hand, it is important that you hold the food properly to prevent cutting your fingers along with the food. Grip the food using the "claw grip" by curling your fingers inward so that you are actually holding the food with your fingernails, keeping your

fingers out of the way of the blade. When this is done properly, the knife will rest against the first knuckles of your fingers, which allows you to make straight, perpendicular cuts more easily while keeping your fingers safe.

Here are some specific instructions for prepping popular produce—avocados, onions, tomatoes, and scallions—that is used frequently in the book's recipes.

HOW TO OPEN AN AVOCADO

While it's simple enough to slice an avocado in half, removing the pit can be a little difficult. But with a little practice, it soon becomes easy.

1. Slice the avocado in half from end to end, and twist to separate the halves.

2. Holding the side with the pit in one hand, cradled by a kitchen towel for safety, use a sharp chef's knife to strike the pit close to the base of the blade so that it lodges in the pit.

3. Twist the knife side to side to dislodge the pit from the avocado. Slide your fingers along the blade of the knife to push the pit off it rather than pulling it, which can be dangerous.

HOW TO DICE AN ONION

This simple technique can be used to cut any kind of onion or shallot. Because of the onion's natural shape in rings, this method allows you to use the rings to form your dice and eliminate one set of cuts that you would otherwise have to do.

1. Using a sharp chef's knife, place the onion on its side, and cut off both ends of the onion. Place one cut-side down on a cutting board with the other facing up.

2. Holding the onion with one hand, place the blade in the middle of the onion so that it is crossing the center circle of the onion's rings. Cut the onion downward into two pieces.

3. Remove the onion's skin, and place both sides center-cut down on the cutting board.

4. Working with one half at a time, cut the onion crosswise into strips parallel with the flat ends of the onion.

5. Flip the rounded strips over, a couple of sections at a time, so that they are stacked up. Position the rounded part facing your guiding hand. Cut downward on the flat edge of the onion with

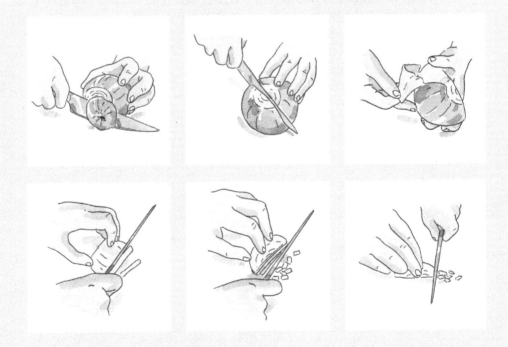

a series of cuts advancing toward your guiding hand to create a dice. Take care with the fingers of your guiding hand as you near the end, as there will not be much room left to hold the onion.

6. At the end, you will have to finish the dicing by chopping the remaining end piece to create dice. Chop the remaining piece or pieces with a couple of crosswise chops to finish the dice.

HOW TO CUT A TOMATO

Tomatoes are easiest to cut with a serrated edge, but a good, sharp chef's knife will do the job. Always be sure to wash and remove any stickers on tomatoes before using them.

For slices:

1. Turn the tomato on its side so that the stem and bottom of the tomato face left and right. If you are a lefty, the stem will face left; otherwise, it will face right.

2. Holding the bottom of the tomato with your guide hand, slice the tomato from stem to bottom into slices of the thickness you want.

For wedges:

1. Lay the tomato on its side on the cutting board so that the stem end is facing away from you.

2. Holding the tomato with your guide hand, make one lengthwise cut through the tomato from stem to base.

3. Place the two pieces cut-side up on the cutting board. Cut each piece through the middle, to separate into two pieces each, making four pieces. Repeat with the four pieces to divide each into two pieces, making a total of eight pieces. If desired, based on the size of the tomato and the recipe, cut the wedges into smaller pieces again by halving each piece.

For dice:

1. Cut a tomato into slices using the earlier method outline.

2. Lay the slices on the cutting board, sliced-side down, stacking up two or three at a time. Cut from one side to another using parallel cuts to create strips.

3. Cut the strips crosswise into a dice.

HOW TO CUT SCALLIONS

Some recipes specify that you use only the white part of a scallion, other recipes, that you use the green part, and sometimes that you use both parts. Be sure to check the recipe to see which part you need before starting. Wash the scallions before using them.

1. Group the scallions together with the root end facing the hand you hold the knife with. Grip the green ends with your guide hand. If you are using only the green part, reverse this positioning.

2. Remove the root end with one perpendicular cut to the base of the scallions and discard.

3. Continue making perpendicular cuts until you have the needed amount. Adjust the cutting width depending on the size needed.

4. Retain the remaining scallions for future recipes, storing them in a plastic bag in the refrigerator.

Chapter 2

GO-TO GREEN SMOOTHIE (PAGE 38)

BREAK-FAST

Go-To Green Smoothie

Serves 1

PREP TIME
5 minutes

**PER SERVING
(1 SMOOTHIE)**
Calories: 285
Fat: 2g
Carbs: 69g
Fiber: 10g
Protein: 8g

prep tip
Blend the fresh ingredients first to release their liquid before adding more water. You may not need as much as you think.

If I could choose only one green smoothie to enjoy for the rest of my life, this is the one. The sweetness of the pineapple and tang of the fresh limes make it a good green smoothie for beginners.

1 lime, peeled
1 cup freshly squeezed orange juice
2 cups roughly chopped kale or spinach
1 cup loosely packed fresh cilantro or parsley
1 cup water
1 cup frozen cubed pineapple

1   Place the lime, orange juice, kale, and cilantro into a blender, and add just enough water to blend. Purée until smooth.

2   Add the frozen pineapple chunks, and blend until smooth.

VARIATIONS

Blueberry Power Greens Smoothie: Blend 2 cups of fresh spinach, 1 banana, and 1 cup of apple juice. Add 1 cup of frozen blueberries, and blend until smooth. If using fresh blueberries, add ½ cup of ice.

Creamy Kale and Banana Smoothie: Blend 2 cups of fresh kale, 1 peeled lime, and 1 cup of almond milk. Add 1 cup of frozen banana chunks, and blend until smooth. If using fresh banana, add ½ cup of ice.

Green Mango Lassi Smoothie: Blend 2 cups of fresh spinach, 1 cup of plain or vanilla yogurt, and ½ cup of water. Add 1 cup of frozen mango chunks, and blend until smooth.

Tropical Breakfast Smoothie

Whether you spent the night studying, finishing a paper, or partying, use this electrolyte-rich smoothie to refresh your body. It is rich in anti-oxidants and may be the perfect way to start the week. Coconut water is a good source of electrolytes; it can be found in the health food or refrigerated beverage section of the grocery store.

1 banana, diced
½ cup frozen pineapple chunks
½ cup frozen mango chunks
1 cup coconut water
1 cup ice

Place the ingredients into the blender in the order listed. Blend until smooth.

VEGAN
GLUTEN-FREE
PREP AND SERVE

Serves 1

PREP TIME
5 minutes

**PER SERVING
(1 SMOOTHIE)**
Calories: 240
Fat: 1g
Carbs: 61g
Fiber: 6g
Protein: 3g

Peanut Butter Cup Smoothie

- VEGAN OPTION
- GLUTEN-FREE
- PREP AND SERVE
- GOOD FOR SHARING

Serves 1

PREP TIME
5 minutes

**PER SERVING
(1 SMOOTHIE)**
Calories: 505
Fat: 22g
Carbs: 66g
Fiber: 6g
Protein: 17g

substitution tip
To make this smoothie vegan, use almond milk instead of cow's milk and opt for 1 tablespoon of unsweetened cocoa powder or a vegan hot chocolate mix.

This smoothie is the answer to the afternoon slump and is so much healthier than anything you could get from a vending machine. It features the timeless flavor combination of peanut butter and chocolate, and tastes like a frozen version of chocolate peanut butter cups. I look forward to some version of this smoothie every afternoon.

¾ **cup 2 percent milk**
2 tablespoons peanut butter
2 tablespoons hot cocoa mix
1 cup frozen banana chunks

Place all the ingredients into the blender, and blend until smooth.

Pumpkin Spice Shake

This recipe is far healthier than the pumpkin milk shakes that pop up every autumn, but it tastes pretty close to those concoctions. For protein, consider adding a scoop of vanilla protein powder. I use a plant-based vanilla protein powder, but whey protein powder is another good option.

½ cup canned pumpkin pie filling
½ cup 2 percent milk
1 banana, diced
1 cup ice

Place the ingredients into the blender in the order listed. Blend until smooth.

substitution tip: For less sugar you can use canned pumpkin purée and add 2 teaspoons of pumpkin pie spice to this shake.

- VEGETARIAN
- GLUTEN-FREE
- PREP AND SERVE

Serves 1

PREP TIME
5 minutes

**PER SERVING
(1 SHAKE)**
Calories: 314
Fat: 3g
Carbs: 69g
Fiber: 14g
Protein: 8g

prep tip
For an extra cool and creamy smoothie, pop the diced banana into the freezer the night before, and use it along with only as much ice as you need to achieve the desired consistency.

Banana Mocha Protein Shake

Serves 1

PREP TIME
5 minutes

**PER SERVING
(1 SHAKE)**
Calories: 316
Fat: 4g
Carbs: 42g
Fiber: 6g
Protein: 27g

prep tip
Freeze leftover coffee in an ice cube tray, and use it in place of the ice in this recipe for an extra jolt of caffeine and flavor.

This smoothie combines complex carbohydrates and protein, making it the perfect postworkout drink. The recipe calls for coffee, and while you can use fresh, hot coffee, yesterday's stale coffee still in the pot will work just fine.

1 banana, diced
1 scoop chocolate protein powder
½ cup 2 percent milk
½ cup coffee
1 cup ice

Place the ingredients into the blender in the order listed. Blend until smooth.

Mason Jar Chia Pudding

When I learned that professional surfer Kelly Slater prefers chia pudding for his morning breakfast, I raced out the door to buy chia seeds and whipped up this yummy vegan recipe. While it didn't make me a better surfer, I did enjoy lasting energy after hours of activity.

1 cup vanilla almond milk or light coconut milk

¼ cup chia seeds

1 cup diced fresh fruit (such as strawberries, mango, or bananas)

OPTIONAL ADD-INS

1 tablespoon nuts (such as almond slivers, chopped walnuts, or chopped pecans)

1 tablespoon coconut flakes

½ tablespoon honey (if using unsweetened almond milk)

1 In a 16-ounce mason jar, add the almond milk, chia seeds, and fruit. If using any add-ins, place them in the jar as well. Screw the lid onto the jar, and shake vigorously.

2 Allow the pudding to rest for 20 minutes before enjoying.

■ VEGAN
■ GLUTEN-FREE
■ PREP AND SERVE

Serves 1

PREP TIME
5 minutes, plus
20 minutes to rest

**PER SERVING
(1 PUDDING)**
Calories: 407
Fat: 20g
Carbs: 51g
Fiber: 25g
Protein: 11g

prep tip
Prepare this recipe the night before by mixing the almond milk and chia seeds in a jar and storing it in the refrigerator to set. Just make sure the chia seeds are distributed throughout the liquid so they don't clump at the bottom. In the morning, add the fruit, and enjoy.

Cinnamon-Raisin Oatmeal

▪ VEGETARIAN
▪ GLUTEN-FREE OPTION
▪ MICROWAVE FRIENDLY

Serves 2

PREP TIME
5 minutes

COOK TIME
7 minutes

PER SERVING
(1¼ CUPS)
Calories: 383
Fat: 9g
Carbs: 70g
Fiber: 6g
Protein: 9g

substitution tip
If you don't have
brown sugar on
hand, substi-
tute cane sugar
in its place.

Sure, you could opt for the instant oatmeal packets. But if you want more than 150 calories and a whole lot less sugar, make your own. It's easier than you think! Make it even easier by popping the whole thing in the microwave for 2 to 3 minutes on high.

1 cup old-fashioned rolled oats
½ cup raisins
1 teaspoon ground cinnamon
Sea salt
1 tablespoon butter
2 teaspoons brown sugar

1 In a small pot, combine the rolled oats, raisins, cinnamon, a small pinch of sea salt, and 2 cups of water. Bring to a simmer over medium heat for 2 minutes.

2 Reduce the heat to low, cover with a lid, and cook for 5 minutes, or until all the water is absorbed and the oats are tender.

3 To serve, top with the butter and brown sugar.

prep tip: If you need to make this gluten-free, buy certi-fied gluten-free oats. Otherwise, there is a possibility of cross-contamination in regular oats.

Cherry-Pecan Oatmeal

Cooking oatmeal in milk yields a rich, creamy texture and adds protein and fat to give you lasting energy. The dried cherries plump up and gently sweeten this decadent breakfast. To toast pecans, heat a dry skillet over medium heat and add the pecans, shaking the pan regularly, for 8 to 10 minutes, until they are fragrant and browned, or microwave them at 1-minute intervals until crisp and fragrant.

1 cup old-fashioned rolled oats, or gluten-free oats

½ cup dried cherries

2 cups whole milk

Sea salt

¼ cup toasted pecan pieces

2 teaspoons brown sugar

1 In a small pot, combine the rolled oats, cherries, milk, and a small pinch of sea salt. Bring to a simmer over medium heat.

2 Reduce the heat to low, cover with a lid, and cook for 5 minutes, or until all the milk is absorbed and the oats are tender.

3 To serve, top with the toasted pecans and brown sugar.

VEGETARIAN

GLUTEN-FREE OPTION

MICROWAVE FRIENDLY

Serves 2

PREP TIME
5 minutes

COOK TIME
7 minutes

PER SERVING
(1¼ CUPS)
Calories: 587
Fat: 19g
Carbs: 88g
Fiber: 8g
Protein: 18g

foodie 101
Brown sugar has a more complex flavor than white sugar, which has been refined to remove molasses.

Basic Scrambled Eggs

VEGETARIAN
GLUTEN-FREE

Serves 2

PREP TIME
5 minutes

COOK TIME
5 to 10 minutes

PER SERVING
(2 EGGS)
Calories: 186
Fat: 14g
Carbs: 1g
Fiber: 0g
Protein: 14g

There's more than one way to scramble an egg, despite what the purists may claim. The traditional method involves cooking whisked eggs slowly, over low heat, stirring constantly to produce a tender scramble. A quicker method is to toss whisked eggs into a searing hot, greased skillet and stir quickly to complete cooking in less than a minute. Either method is acceptable, but always remove the pan from the heat just before the eggs are done to ensure they don't overcook. I prefer to cook eggs somewhere in between, at medium heat.

½ tablespoon butter
4 eggs, whisked
Sea salt
Freshly ground black pepper

1 Heat a skillet over medium heat until warmed. Add the butter, and tilt the pan to coat as it melts.

2 Pour the eggs into the pan, and season with salt.

3 Use a silicone spatula to stir the eggs, making contact with the pan as you go to ensure none of the eggs remain on the pan surface for too long.

4 Continue stirring for about 5 minutes, until the eggs are nearly cooked through and set. Remove the pan from the heat, and serve with freshly ground pepper.

Cheesy Egg Scramble: Follow the basic instructions. Fold in ½ cup of shredded sharp Cheddar cheese just before removing the eggs from the stove.

Spicy Ham Scramble: Follow the basic instructions. Fold in ½ cup of diced ham and a pinch of red pepper flakes just before removing the eggs from the stove.

South of the Border Scramble: Follow the basic instructions. Just before removing the eggs from the stove, fold in ¼ cup of shredded pepper Jack cheese and ½ cup of drained and rinsed black beans. Serve with Fresh Salsa (page 190) and 5-Minute Guacamole (page 188).

Mediterranean Scramble: Follow the basic instructions. Just before the eggs set, add ¼ cup of diced tomato, 2 tablespoons of sliced black olives, and 2 tablespoons of crumbled feta cheese to the pan. Continue to cook until heated through.

serving tip
For eggs on the go, wrap the scrambled eggs in a warmed, medium flour tortilla for a very basic breakfast burrito. Adding a little shredded Cheddar cheese or mashing half an avocado in the wrap will add flavor and prevent the eggs from falling out of the tortilla.

ingredient tip
For almost double the protein and half the fat, use 2 eggs and 6 egg whites, then follow the instructions.

How to Cook Eggs

While this cookbook offers recipes to help you cook a variety of meals and snacks, the reality is that most of us tend to eat the same things over and over. If you fall into this category, the almighty egg is a great food to get familiar with. You can cook it in a variety of ways; you can combine it with vegetables (or not—you choose), and it never takes very long to prepare. My scrambled eggs recipe is on the preceding pages, and here are four other basic egg preparations to master.

OMELET

An omelet can be stuffed or have ingredients cooked right into it. It can be circular or a half moon. Whatever you prefer, the basic premise is that an omelet is made by frying beaten eggs in a frying pan. To make a simple omelet, follow these instructions:

1. In a small bowl, whisk 2 eggs. Season with salt and pepper.

2. Heat a large skillet over medium-high heat until hot. Add ¼ tablespoon butter or ½ tablespoon oil and continue to heat for 30 seconds.

3. Pour the eggs into the pan, and tilt it to coat the bottom of the pan.

4. When the eggs begin to set around the edges, lift one of the edges gently with a spatula, and tilt the pan to allow some of the raw egg on top to slide down under the omelet. Repeat on the other sides of the omelet.

5. When the top is nearly set, add toppings such as cheese, diced vegetables, herbs, or cooked meat.

6. Carefully lift one side of the omelet and fold it over the fillings. Press down on the edges gently to seal. Cook for 1 minute. Using a spatula, flip the omelet onto the opposite side. Cook for 1 minute more, or until the egg is set and the fillings are heated through.

SOFT- OR HARD-BOILED EGGS

Soft-boiled eggs, like other eggs, are great for breakfast, and delicious in a bowl of soup or with potatoes. When the egg is split, the yolk of a soft-boiled egg will be runny. Depending on how long you cook the eggs, the whites range from slightly runny to completely set, as in a hard-boiled egg. Add hard-boiled eggs to salads and sandwiches, or simply sprinkle with salt and pepper to eat.

1. In a small pot, cover 4 eggs with cold water.

2. Bring to a boil over medium heat.

3. Soft-boil or hard-boil the eggs.

For soft-boiled eggs

Remove from the heat, cover, and let them sit for 5 to 7 minutes in the hot water. An egg cooked for 5 minutes will be rather runny, while one cooked for 7 minutes will still have a runny yolk but will be more firmly set.

For hard-boiled eggs

Remove from the heat, cover, and let them sit for 12 minutes in the hot water.

With tongs or a slotted spoon, transfer the eggs to a bowl filled with ice water to stop the cooking process. Store the eggs peeled or unpeeled in the refrigerator.

To peel, tap the egg gently against a clean, hard surface such as the counter or sink to break the shell, and peel the shell away with your hands.

POACHED EGGS

Poaching an egg uses no added fat, making it a healthy and simple way to prepare an egg. Serve poached eggs over toast, on pizzas, or in a bowl of ramen.

1. Fill a small pot with about 2 inches of cold water. Bring the water to a gentle simmer.

2. Carefully crack an egg into a small bowl. Gently pour the egg from the bowl into the simmering water. Quickly move the white over the yolk with a wooden spoon. Allow the egg to cook for 3 to 5 minutes, until the whites are set. With a slotted spoon, transfer the poached egg to a serving dish.

Potato-Onion Frittata

■ VEGETARIAN
■ GLUTEN-FREE

Serves 2

PREP TIME
5 minutes

COOK TIME
25 minutes

PER SERVING
(½ FRITTATA)
Calories: 380
Fat: 18g
Carbs: 37g
Fiber: 3g
Protein: 18g

serving tip
This recipe is similar to the classic Spanish tapa "tortilla," which is often served with aioli. Make your own by whisking together ¼ cup of mayonnaise, 1 teaspoon of minced garlic, ¼ teaspoon of cayenne pepper, and 1 tablespoon of lemon juice.

This recipe yields two servings for breakfast. If you're making it for dinner or you have a big appetite, you may want to enjoy the whole thing yourself. If not, simply wrap the leftovers, refrigerate, and microwave for about 45 seconds the next day.

1 tablespoon extra-virgin olive oil
1 medium russet potato, unpeeled, thinly sliced in rounds
1 small yellow onion, thinly sliced
4 eggs, whisked
¼ teaspoon sea salt
Freshly ground black pepper

1   In a large skillet, heat the olive oil over medium heat. Add the potato and onion, and cook for 15 minutes, stirring often, until the potato is nearly soft.

2   In a small bowl, combine the eggs and salt. Stir to combine. Pour the eggs in the pan, and cook, undisturbed for an additional 8 minutes, until the top is set.

3   Slice into wedges and serve.

prep tip: Speed up the cooking time by piercing the whole potato with a fork and microwaving it on high for 3 minutes. Slice it into thin rounds, and use 2 thinly sliced scallions instead of yellow onion. Add the potatoes, scallions, and eggs to the hot skillet at the same time. Cook for 5 minutes on the stove top, and transfer to the oven to cook for another 5 minutes at 400°F.

Southwestern Skillet

This is one of my favorite breakfasts, and it's perfect for using up extra vegetables you may have lying around. Don't have sweet potatoes? Swap them for potatoes or zucchini or whatever you have on hand. The scramble is delicious on its own, or serve it with corn chips or wrapped in a corn tortilla.

1 tablespoon extra-virgin olive oil
1 small sweet potato, unpeeled, finely diced
1 small green bell pepper, cored and diced
¼ cup corn kernels, fresh or thawed if frozen
4 eggs, whisked
Sea salt
Freshly ground black pepper
½ cup roasted tomato salsa

1 In a large skillet, heat the olive oil over medium heat. Add the sweet potato, and cook for 12 minutes, stirring often, until nearly soft.

2 Add the bell pepper, and cook for 5 minutes, until the peppers become slightly softened.

3 Add the corn kernels, and cook for 1 minute.

4 Pour in the eggs, stirring constantly in a circular motion, and cook for about 5 minutes, until the eggs are set. Season with salt and pepper.

5 Top with the tomato salsa to serve.

■ VEGETARIAN
■ GLUTEN-FREE

Serves 2

PREP TIME
5 minutes

COOK TIME
25 minutes

PER SERVING
(½ SKILLET)
Calories: 340
Fat: 18g
Carbs: 28g
Fiber: 4g
Protein: 18g

prep tip
To remove the corn from the cob, remove the corn husks, stand the ear on one end, and use a sharp knife to shave down each side.

Granola

Granola has outgrown its hippie roots, and the good stuff can cost several dollars per serving. Ouch! Learning how to make your own can save you big bucks. Plus, you can fill it with your favorite ingredients. Here's the basic version. Feel free to add other dried fruits, coconut, or vanilla extract.

■ VEGETARIAN
■ GLUTEN-FREE OPTION
■ GOOD FOR SHARING

Serves 6

PREP TIME
5 minutes

COOK TIME
25 minutes

PER SERVING (ABOUT 1 CUP)
Calories: 652
Fat: 32g
Carbs: 85g
Fiber: 10g
Protein: 12g

prep tip
Make sure to set the timer! Granola burns easily.

3 cups old-fashioned oats, or gluten-free oats
1½ cups chopped nuts or seeds, such as pecans, walnuts, almonds, sunflower seeds, or pepitas
½ cup canola oil
¼ teaspoon sea salt
½ cup brown sugar
1 egg white, whisked
1 cup dried cranberries or raisins

1 Preheat the oven to 350°F.

2 Spread out the oats and nuts on a rimmed baking sheet.

3 In a large measuring cup, whisk together the oil, sea salt, sugar, and egg white. Pour this over the oats and nuts, and use your hands to mix thoroughly. Flatten the oats with your hands, packing the mixture down gently onto the baking sheet.

4 Bake for 10 minutes. Flip the granola over with a metal spatula, and pat down again. Bake for another 10 minutes. Flip the granola again, trying not to break up the larger pieces. Bake for another 5 minutes.

5 Allow to cool completely, then add the cranberries. Store in a container.

Ham and Cheese Breakfast Sandwich

This hot and toasty breakfast sandwich is easy to pull together in just a few minutes on your way out the door. It has the protein, carbs, and fat to keep you energized through all your morning classes. You can purchase packaged sliced cheese and ham separately, or visit the deli counter to order just the amount you need.

1 tablespoon canola oil
1 egg
Sea salt
Freshly ground black pepper
2 slices Cheddar cheese
1 English muffin
2 slices Black Forest ham or Canadian bacon

1 In a large skillet, heat the oil over medium-high heat. Crack the egg into a small bowl, and pour into the pan. Cook the egg for 2 minutes. Season with salt and pepper. Carefully flip the egg, trying not to break the yolk. Top the egg with the sliced Cheddar cheese, and cook for 1 minute.

2 While the egg cooks, toast the English muffin in a toaster oven.

3 Place the ham on the bottom slice of the English muffin. Top with the egg and cheese, and close with the top half of the English muffin.

■ **GLUTEN-FREE OPTION**

Serves 1

PREP TIME
2 minutes

COOK TIME
5 minutes

PER SERVING (1 MUFFIN SANDWICH)
Calories: 612
Fat: 41g
Carbs: 30g
Fiber: 2g
Protein: 32g

substitution tip
To make this gluten-free, use gluten-free English muffins or a corn tortilla to make this a yummy wrap.

Classic French Toast

■ VEGETARIAN

■ GOOD FOR
  SHARING

Serves 4

PREP TIME
5 minutes

COOK TIME
15 minutes

PER SERVING
(2 PIECES)
Calories: 328
Fat: 11g
Carbs: 43g
Fiber: 1g
Protein: 10g

French toast was one of the first things I learned to cook. It's easy because it doesn't really require you to measure your ingredients; just whisk together the eggs and milk, dip the bread in the mixture, and fry it up. This recipe is easily multiplied to serve a crowd as part of brunch. While this classic breakfast dish is easily cooked on the stove top, you might consider the baked variation provided afterward if you'd prefer a hands-off approach.

2 eggs
¾ cup 2 percent milk
8 large slices white bread or challah
2 tablespoons butter, plus more for serving
¼ cup maple syrup, for serving

1   Whisk together the eggs and milk in a large shallow baking dish. Place all the bread slices in the dish, and flip them to soak up the liquid on both sides.

2   Heat a large skillet over medium heat until hot. Add about one-quarter of the butter to the pan, and tilt to coat the pan.

3   When the butter is melted, remove a couple of slices of bread from the egg mixture, shaking to remove any excess liquid. Cook on each side for about 2 minutes, or until golden brown. Transfer to a serving plate, and repeat with the remaining butter and slices of bread.

4   Serve with additional butter and maple syrup.

VARIATIONS

Raspberry-Almond French Toast: Top each serving of French toast with 1 tablespoon of raspberry preserves and 1 tablespoon of sliced or slivered almonds.

Peanut Butter–Banana French Toast: Top each serving of French toast with 1 tablespoon of peanut butter and ¼ cup of sliced bananas. Drizzle with maple syrup.

Baked French Toast: Coat an 8-by-8-inch baking dish with 1 tablespoon of butter. Layer the bread slices into the dish, and pour the egg and milk mixture over them, turning them to coat the bread slices. Bake at 325°F for 25 minutes.

leftovers tip
Freeze individual slices of cooked French toast in zip-top plastic bags. When you're ready to serve, remove them from the bag, and pop them into a toaster oven to warm.

AVOCADO TOAST WITH
POACHED EGG AND
TOMATO SALAD
(PAGE 59)

Chapter 3

SNACKS AND SMALL BITES

Creamy Avocado Toast

■ VEGETARIAN

Serves 2

PREP TIME
5 minutes

COOK TIME
2 minutes

**PER SERVING
(1 TOAST)**
Calories: 337
Fat: 21g
Carbs: 32g
Fiber: 11g
Protein: 3g

Avocado is a convenient, inexpensive, and healthy snack option loaded with brain-boosting monounsaturated fats. The fruit—yes, it's a fruit—is also incredibly versatile, and pairs well with tomatoes, cucumber, bacon, cheese, and herbs. This version is extra-creamy because it calls for cream cheese, but simply remove it for a just-as-delicious vegan variation.

2 slices whole-wheat bread
2 tablespoons cream cheese
1 small avocado, pitted and sliced
1 ripe tomato, thinly sliced
Sea salt
Freshly ground black pepper
1 teaspoon red wine vinegar (optional)

1 Toast the bread in a toaster oven.

2 Top each slice with 1 tablespoon of cream cheese and half of the avocado and tomato slices. Season with salt and pepper and a sprinkle of red wine vinegar (if using).

Avocado Toast with Poached Egg and Tomato Salad: Mash 1 avocado and spread it over two slices of whole grain toast. Top each with 1 poached egg (see page 49 for poaching instructions). For the tomato salad, combine 1 cup halved cherry tomatoes with 1 teaspoon red wine vinegar, 1 teaspoon extra-virgin olive oil, and a pinch of sea salt. Garnish with minced fresh parsley.

Avocado-Chicken Open-Face Sandwich: Dice 1 avocado, and mix with 1 cup of diced, cooked chicken breast, 1 tablespoon of lime juice, and 1 tablespoon of minced fresh basil (optional). Season with salt and pepper. Divide the mixture between 2 slices of toasted whole-wheat bread.

Avocado-Bacon Toast: Top 2 slices of toasted whole-wheat bread with the slices of 1 avocado and 2 slices, halved, of cooked bacon.

Sweet Potato Fries with Chipotle Mayo

Serves 2 to 4

PREP TIME
5 minutes

COOK TIME
25 minutes

PER SERVING
Calories: 483
Fat: 34g
Carbs: 42g
Fiber: 7g
Protein: 4g

foodie 101
Chipotle peppers in adobo is smoked, dried jalapeño peppers in a tangy red sauce. Look for chipotle peppers in adobo in the Mexican foods aisle in your grocery store.

If you're accustomed to deep-fried sweet potatoes, prepare to be amazed. Oven roasting makes sweet potatoes even more delicious because the starches and sugars in the vegetable caramelize. The sweet earthiness of the fries paired with the tangy, spicy mayo is absolutely addicting, and these will vanish in minutes.

3 small sweet potatoes, unpeeled
2 tablespoons canola oil
Sea salt
¼ cup mayonnaise
1 tablespoon freshly squeezed lemon juice
1 tablespoon minced chipotle peppers in adobo sauce

1. Preheat the oven to 400°F.

2. Slice the sweet potatoes lengthwise into ½-inch-thick pieces. Spread the pieces out on a rimmed baking sheet, and drizzle with oil. Toss gently with your hands to coat the sweet potatoes in the oil. Season with sea salt.

3. Roast for 25 minutes, or until the sweet potatoes are browned on the bottoms and soft.

4. Meanwhile, whisk together the mayonnaise, lemon juice, and chipotle peppers in a small bowl. Refrigerate until you're ready to serve.

5. Transfer the cooked sweet potato fries to a serving bowl, and serve with the chipotle mayo.

Roasted Squash with Lemon-Garlic Yogurt

Delicata squash, which is cream colored with orange and green streaks, shows up at markets in the fall. As the name suggests, the skin of the squash is delicate and can be eaten, saving you from the annoying prep step of peeling the outer skin. In fact, it adds a delicious textural contrast. You can also use kabocha or acorn squash, but you would then need to increase the cooking time by 10 minutes.

1 delicata squash, halved lengthwise and seeded

2 tablespoons extra-virgin olive oil

Sea salt

Zest and juice of 1 lemon

1 garlic clove, minced

¼ cup plain yogurt

1 Preheat the oven to 400°F.

2 Slice the squash halves crosswise into ½-inch-thick slices. They should have a C shape when sliced correctly. Spread them out onto a rimmed baking sheet. Drizzle with the olive oil, and toss gently to coat. Season with salt.

3 Roast for 20 minutes.

4 Meanwhile, in a small bowl, whisk together the lemon zest and juice, garlic, and yogurt. Refrigerate until you're ready to serve.

5 Transfer the cooked squash to a serving bowl, and serve with the lemon-garlic yogurt.

■ VEGETARIAN
■ GLUTEN-FREE

Serves 2

PREP TIME
5 minutes

COOK TIME
20 minutes

PER SERVING
(½ SQUASH, PLUS
2 TABLESPOONS
OF YOGURT)
Calories: 288
Fat: 20g
Carbs: 29g
Fiber: 9g
Protein: 5g

leftovers tip
If you have leftover roasted squash, cut it into medium-size chunks and add them to a mixed green salad with cooked chicken breast. Drizzle with any remaining lemon-garlic yogurt.

Kung Pao Chickpeas

■ VEGAN
■ MICROWAVE
 FRIENDLY
■ GOOD FOR
 SHARING

Serves 4

PREP TIME
5 minutes

COOK TIME
10 minutes

PER SERVING
(ABOUT 1 CUP)
Calories: 456
Fat: 23g
Carbs: 52g
Fiber: 9g
Protein: 14g

Usually vegetarian versions of Chinese food go straight to soy—tempeh or tofu. This savory homemade takeout uses chickpeas instead. They're a good source of protein and complex carbohydrates and soak up the kung pao sauce. Serve on a bed of rice, and top with some thinly sliced scallions for color.

2 tablespoons canola oil
2 (15-ounce) cans chickpeas, drained
2 garlic cloves, minced
1 teaspoon minced ginger
¾ cup kung pao sauce
½ cup toasted cashews

1 In a large skillet, heat the oil over medium heat. Cook the chickpeas for 2 to 3 minutes, until heated through and beginning to brown. Add the garlic and ginger, and cook for another 30 seconds.

2 Add the kung pao sauce, and cook for 5 minutes.

3 Stir in the cashews.

foodie 101: The liquid found in canned chickpeas is called aquafaba and can be used as a thickener. Make a vegan mayonnaise with 3 tablespoons of aquafaba, 1 tablespoon of vinegar, ½ teaspoon of sea salt, and 1 cup of canola oil. Combine all the ingredients except the oil, and whisk to combine. Slowly drizzle in the oil a few drops at a time, whisking constantly until it is emulsified.

ingredient tip
The Chinese-food chain restaurant Panda Express makes a commercially available kung pao sauce, but if you can't find it, feel free to replace it with a stir-fry sauce. It won't offer the same spicy kick, but it'll do.

No-Bake Energy Balls

Many homemade energy balls rely on a food processor to finely chop nuts and dates into a homogenous mixture. This version uses almond butter and barely melted chocolate to hold things together. Just be sure to chop the nuts and cranberries as finely as you can with your chef's knife.

½ cup almond butter

¼ cup brown sugar

¼ teaspoon sea salt

1 cup finely chopped nuts and seeds, such as walnuts, almonds, sunflower seeds, or pepitas

1 cup finely chopped dried cranberries

1 cup roughly chopped dark chocolate chips

1 In a small microwave-safe bowl, combine the almond butter, brown sugar, and sea salt, and microwave on high for 30 seconds. Stir and microwave on high for another 30 seconds, or until the mixture is hot and the brown sugar and salt are dissolved.

2 In a medium mixing bowl, combine the nuts, cranberries, and chocolate chips. Pour the hot almond butter mixture into the bowl, and stir to mix. The heat from the almond butter will melt the chocolate pieces somewhat.

3 Scoop the nut mixture into 1-inch balls, and pack the balls with your hands. Place them on the baking sheet, and refrigerate until set. Store in a covered container in the refrigerator.

- VEGAN
- GLUTEN-FREE
- MICROWAVE FRIENDLY
- PREP AND SERVE
- GOOD FOR SHARING

Yields 2 dozen

PREP TIME
10 minutes, plus time to chill

COOK TIME
1 minute

PER SERVING (2 BALLS)
Calories: 243
Fat: 15g
Carbs: 29g
Fiber: 4g
Protein: 5g

substitution tip
If you prefer to use a natural sweetener, you can use honey, maple syrup, or agave nectar in place of the brown sugar. If you opt for agave nectar, use only 3 tablespoons.

Yogurt Bark

Serves 4

PREP TIME
5 minutes, plus 1 to
2 hours to freeze

**PER SERVING
(ABOUT 1 CUP)**
Calories: 388
Fat: 20g
Carbs: 47g
Fiber: 8g
Protein: 9g

leftovers tip
This snack also
makes an excellent
on-the-go breakfast;
just be sure to wrap
it in a paper towel to
keep the yogurt from
melting onto your
fingers.

If you live in an apartment with roommates or a dorm with a shared freezer, you may want to find the deepest corner of that freezer to stash this creamy frozen treat. It is so delicious, everyone will want a piece! Use any fruit you like—mangos, strawberries, and raspberries all work well.

2 cups vanilla yogurt
½ cup thinly sliced almonds or slivered almonds
1 cup fresh blueberries
1 cup Granola (page 52) or store bought

1 Line a rimmed baking sheet with parchment paper. Spread the yogurt in a ¼- to ½-inch-thick layer on the parchment paper.

2 Sprinkle the almonds and blueberries onto the yogurt, then sprinkle with the granola.

3 Freeze for 1 to 2 hours, or until set. Break the yogurt into pieces and enjoy.

Honey-Yogurt Fruit Dip

Fruit is lovely on its own, but for a more filling snack, pair it with protein-rich Greek yogurt. I prefer starting with plain yogurt so that I can choose how much sweetener to add. However, you could opt for honey vanilla yogurt, and stir in the lemon zest to make it even easier.

1 cup plain Greek yogurt

¼ cup honey, warmed

1 teaspoon vanilla extract

¼ teaspoon lemon zest

2 cups assorted fruit, such as sliced apple, strawberries, pineapple, and melon

In a small bowl, combine the yogurt, honey, vanilla, and lemon zest, and stir. Serve topped with the assorted fruit.

▪ **VEGETARIAN**
▪ **GLUTEN-FREE**
▪ **PREP AND SERVE**

Serves 2

PREP TIME
5 minutes

PER SERVING
(1½ CUPS)
Calories: 259
Fat: 1g
Carbs: 57g
Fiber: 3g
Protein: 12g

foodie 101
Greek yogurt is made in the same manner as traditional yogurt, but it is strained to remove some of the liquid. This gives Greek yogurt more protein than other varieties.

Peanut Butter Yogurt Spread

- VEGETARIAN
- GLUTEN-FREE
- PREP AND SERVE
- GOOD FOR SHARING

Serves 4

PREP TIME
5 minutes

PER SERVING
(2 RICE CAKES WITH
½ CUP SPREAD)
Calories: 414
Fat: 22g
Carbs: 42g
Fiber: 4g
Protein: 16g

Enjoy this peanut butter yogurt studded with chocolate chips as a topping for rice cakes, as served here, or use it as a dip for apple slices, or just eat it with a spoon. Sure, it's loaded with satisfying protein and healthy fats, but its addicting sweet and savory flavors will keep you coming back for bite after bite.

1 cup vanilla Greek yogurt
½ cup creamy peanut butter
½ cup mini chocolate chips
8 rice cakes

In a small mixing bowl, combine the yogurt, peanut butter, and chocolate chips, and mix thoroughly. Divide the mixture between the rice cakes, and serve immediately.

leftovers tip: Store leftover peanut butter yogurt and rice cakes separately to keep the rice cakes from getting soggy.

Spinach and Artichoke Dip

Spinach and artichoke dip is on appetizer menus for a reason—it's really delicious. You can dip bread slices or tortilla chips into it, or even cut vegetables. This quick and easy version turns out great in the oven or microwave.

1 teaspoon canola oil

1 (15-ounce) can artichoke hearts, drained and roughly chopped

2 cups roughly chopped fresh spinach

2 garlic cloves, minced

8 ounces cream cheese, cut into 1-inch cubes

1 cup grated mozzarella cheese

Sea salt

Freshly ground black pepper

1 Preheat the oven to 325°F. Coat the interior of a baking dish with oil.

2 In the baking dish, layer the oil, artichoke hearts, spinach, garlic, cream cheese, and mozzarella cheese in the order listed, and season with salt and pepper.

3 Bake uncovered for 20 minutes, or until the cheese is browned and bubbling. Stir before serving.

prep tip: To make this in the microwave, place all the ingredients in a microwave-safe dish and microwave on high for 1 minute. Stir, and microwave for another minute, until the cheese is melted.

- VEGETARIAN
- GLUTEN-FREE
- MICROWAVE-FRIENDLY
- GOOD FOR SHARING

Serves 4

PREP TIME
5 minutes

COOK TIME
20 minutes

PER SERVING
(¾ CUP)
Calories: 357
Fat: 27g
Carbs: 16g
Fiber: 4g
Protein: 14g

Creamy Salsa Verde Taquitos

Serves 4

PREP TIME
5 minutes

COOK TIME
5 minutes

PER SERVING (3 TAQUITOS)
Calories: 513
Fat: 36g
Carbs: 37g
Fiber: 0g
Protein: 12g

prep tip
If the corn tortillas are not pliable, microwave them individually for 10 seconds before filling.

These crispy, creamy bites are perfect game-day snacks or fuel for late-night study sessions. This homemade version is baked instead of fried, providing a healthier alternative for this classic snacking favorite. For more protein, add 8 ounces of shredded chicken to the mixture.

8 ounces cream cheese
1 cup Monterey Jack cheese
1 cup salsa verde, plus more for serving
1 teaspoon smoked paprika (optional)
12 corn tortillas
2 tablespoons canola oil

1 Preheat the oven to 400°F.

2 In a medium bowl, combine the cream cheese, Monterey Jack cheese, salsa verde, and smoked paprika (if using). Spoon ¼ cup of the mixture into each tortilla, and roll into a tight cylinder. Place seam-side down on a rimmed baking tray.

3 Brush the tortillas with the oil. Bake for 15 minutes, until gently browned and the filling is oozing. Allow to rest for 5 minutes before serving with additional salsa verde for dipping.

Bacon-Wrapped Dates

Everything is better with bacon. In this classic appetizer recipe, bacon provides the perfect smoky flavor to complement sweet dates, complex cheese, and crunchy almonds. Don't want to futz with buying more than two ingredients? Skip the cheese and almonds. Just wrap the dates in bacon and call it good.

16 fresh dates, pitted

8 slices bacon (not thick cut), halved crosswise

16 almond slivers

2 ounces hard cheese, such as Manchego or Parmesan, cut into 16 pieces

1   Preheat the oven to 325°F.

2   Stuff each of the dates with 1 almond sliver and 1 piece of cheese, closing the date around the filling.

3   Wrap 1 bacon slice around each date, and place seam-side down on a rimmed baking sheet.

4   Bake for 20 minutes, or until the bacon has rendered its fat and is beginning to brown.

■ GLUTEN-FREE
■ GOOD FOR SHARING

Serves 4

PREP TIME
10 minutes

COOK TIME
20 minutes

PER SERVING (4 DATES)
Calories: 478
Fat: 17g
Carbs: 74g
Fiber: 7g
Protein: 15g

foodie 101
Manchego is a sheep's milk cheese from Spain. It is the perfect addition to any appetizer platter. It doesn't melt like other cheeses do, so it will stay inside the date during baking.

Bruschetta

VEGAN

GOOD FOR
SHARING

Serves 4

PREP TIME
5 minutes

COOK TIME
5 minutes

PER SERVING
(2 PIECES OF
BAGUETTE PLUS
½ CUP TOPPING)
Calories: 268
Fat: 15g
Carbs: 27g
Fiber: 4g
Protein: 6g

In college I worked at an Italian restaurant where we served bruschetta (*bru-sket-uh*). The recipe is so easy to replicate and far less expensive than most restaurants charge. It is also highly adaptable, so you can swap the tomatoes and basil for figs, goat cheese, and honey, or whatever sounds appetizing.

1 pint grape or cherry tomatoes, halved
¼ cup roughly chopped fresh basil
2 tablespoons balsamic vinegar
Sea salt
Freshly ground black pepper
4 tablespoons extra-virgin olive oil, divided
8 slices crusty baguette

1 In a small mixing bowl, combine the tomatoes, basil, and balsamic vinegar. Season with salt and pepper. Set aside to allow the flavors to come together.

2 In a large skillet, heat 2 tablespoons of oil over medium heat. Add 4 slices of bread, and fry for 2 minutes on each side, or until golden brown. Transfer to a serving platter.

3 Fry the remaining bread slices in the same manner, using the remaining 2 tablespoons of oil, and transfer to the serving platter.

4 Top each of the bread slices with the tomato-basil mixture, and serve immediately.

Mozzarella Sticks

A staple on appetizer menus, these savory cheese sticks are a crowd favorite. So make up a batch when you're hosting study sessions, or bring them to game-day parties. However, unlike the bar food, this version is baked, not deep-fried.

8 (1-ounce) packaged string cheese sticks, halved crosswise
1 egg, whisked
1 cup herbed bread crumbs
1 cup prepared marinara sauce or marinara sauce from
    Spaghetti Marinara (page 112), warmed

1 Preheat the oven to 425°F. Line a rimmed baking sheet with parchment paper.

2 Dip each of the string cheese pieces into the egg, and shake off any excess. Roll in the bread crumbs to coat, and arrange on the baking sheet so that the pieces are not touching.

3 Bake for 15 minutes, or until the cheese is beginning to melt and the bread crumbs are lightly browned.

4 Serve with the marinara sauce for dipping.

■ **VEGETARIAN**
■ **MICROWAVE FRIENDLY**
■ **GOOD FOR SHARING**

Serves 4

PREP TIME
5 minutes

COOK TIME
15 minutes

PER SERVING (2 STICKS)
Calories: 311
Fat: 13g
Carbs: 30g
Fiber: 3g
Protein: 21g

prep tip
To make these in the microwave, place them on a microwave-safe platter, and cook for 1 to 2 minutes, or until the cheese is melty.

Thai Lettuce Cups

▪ GLUTEN-FREE
▪ GOOD FOR
   SHARING

Serves 4

PREP TIME
5 minutes

COOK TIME
6 minutes

PER SERVING
(½ CUP CHICKEN,
LETTUCE, AND
2 TABLESPOONS OF
DIPPING SAUCE)
Calories: 231
Fat: 11g
Carbs: 7g
Fiber: 2g
Protein: 26g

---

prep tip
If you have a box
grater or a Micro-
plane grater, use
it to prepare the
garlic and ginger for
this recipe. If not,
a chef's knife also
works well.

I love ordering lettuce wraps at Thai restaurants, mostly because I love the tangy peanut sauce that accompanies them. Fortunately, the sauce is easily obtained in the Asian section of most grocery stores. Or you can make your own Thai Peanut Sauce (page 129).

1 tablespoon canola oil
1 pound boneless, skinless chicken thighs, minced
Sea salt
Freshly ground black pepper
1 tablespoon minced ginger
1 tablespoon minced garlic
1 head butter lettuce
½ cup Thai Peanut Sauce (page 129) or store bought, for serving

OPTIONAL ADD-INS
1 cup shredded carrots
½ cup roughly chopped cilantro leaves
½ cup thinly sliced red onions

1 In a large skillet, heat the oil over medium-high heat.

2 Season the chicken with salt and pepper. Add to the skillet, and fry until cooked through, about 5 minutes.

3 Add the ginger and garlic to the pan, and cook for another 30 seconds, until they are just fragrant.

4 Divide the chicken between the lettuce leaves, and top with add-ins (if using). Serve with the peanut sauce for dipping.

Stuffed Mushrooms

Stuffed mushrooms are a delicious vegetarian appetizer to serve when friends are over. If you really like mushrooms, you can also use two large portobello mushrooms to make this into a filling entrée and the star of the meal.

2 shallots, minced
8 ounces cream cheese
½ cup bread crumbs
1 tablespoon chopped fresh thyme leaves
Sea salt
Freshly ground black pepper
12 cremini or button mushrooms

1 Preheat the oven to 400°F.

2 In a small mixing bowl, combine the shallots, cream cheese, bread crumbs, and thyme. Season the mixture with salt and pepper, and stir well.

3 Remove the stems from the mushrooms, and rinse the caps under cool running water and pat dry with paper towels.

4 Divide the cream cheese mixture between the mushroom caps, and place them filling-side up on a rimmed baking sheet. Bake for 8 to 10 minutes.

substitution tip: If you don't have fresh thyme, use 1 teaspoon of dried thyme or an equal amount of any other fresh or dried herbs such as rosemary, parsley, or basil.

■ VEGETARIAN
■ GOOD FOR SHARING

Serves 4

PREP TIME
5 minutes

COOK TIME
8 to 10 minutes

PER SERVING
(3 MUSHROOMS)
Calories: 268
Fat: 21g
Carbs: 16g
Fiber: 1g
Protein: 7g

prep tip
Mushrooms are very absorbent, but they won't soak up water when they're patted dry after they're rinsed.

CAPRESE SALAD
(PAGE 81)

Chapter 4

SALADS AND SAND- WICHES

Everyday Kale Salad

■ VEGAN
■ GLUTEN-FREE
■ PREP AND SERVE
■ GOOD FOR SHARING

Serves 2

PREP TIME
10 minutes

PER SERVING
(1 CUP)
Calories: 219
Fat: 22g
Carbs: 8g
Fiber: 3g
Protein: 2g

Kale has become the celebrity of leafy greens and for good reason. It is sturdier than lettuce, is a good plant source of protein, and has a sweet flavor and firm texture. It also plays well with other ingredients, serving as a delicious backdrop to spicy, savory, and subtle flavors. Use a good-quality olive oil when making this salad—its flavor really shines through in the raw preparation.

1 bunch kale, tough ribs removed
1 garlic clove, minced
Pinch red pepper flakes
Zest and juice of 1 lemon
1 tablespoon red wine vinegar
3 tablespoons extra-virgin olive oil
Sea salt
Freshly ground black pepper

1 Roughly chop the kale into bite-size pieces.

2 In a large bowl, combine the garlic, red pepper flakes, lemon zest and juice, and red wine vinegar.

3 Pour in the olive oil in a thin, steady stream, whisking constantly until the dressing emulsifies. Season with salt and pepper.

4 With clean hands, add the kale to the bowl and mix, massaging the dressing into the leaves of the kale to coat. The kale will release some of its liquid and soften as you do this. Serve immediately.

prep tip
To remove the stems from kale leaves, grasp the kale stem firmly with one hand. With the opposite hand, slide your fingers down the length of the stem, pulling the leaf off as you go.

VARIATIONS

Kale, Pear, and Pecan Salad: Whisk together 1 minced shallot, 1 tablespoon of red wine vinegar, and 2 tablespoons of extra-virgin olive oil. Season with salt and pepper. Toss the kale in the dressing, and top with 1 sliced pear and 2 tablespoons of toasted pecans.

Kale Caesar Salad: Drizzle ½ cup of Creamy Caesar Dressing (page 194) over the kale, and toss gently to mix. Top with ½ cup of grated Parmesan cheese, and serve with lemon wedges.

Asian Kale Salad: Drizzle ½ cup of Sesame-Ginger Dressing (page 195) over the kale, and toss gently to mix. Top with ¼ cup of almond slices, ½ cup of canned mandarin orange segments, and ¼ cup of thinly sliced green onions.

foodie 101
The three varieties of kale you're most likely to see at the grocery store are Lacinato, green, and purple. Lacinato kale, also called cavolo nero or Tuscan kale, has a dark green, matte leaf with a thick, bubbled texture. Green and purple kales have a curly leaf and are, as their names suggest, green or purple. Use whatever variety suits your taste.

Sesame-Ginger Chopped Salad

Serves 4

PREP TIME
5 minutes

PER SERVING
(½ CUP)
Calories: 268
Fat: 15g
Carbs: 27g
Fiber: 4g
Protein: 6g

foodie 101
Cilantro is one of the most widely used herbs in the world, but some people just don't like it. If you're one of them, use fresh mint or basil instead.

This tangy side salad is loaded with flavor. Crisp cabbage and carrots, cilantro, and scallions are coated in a spicy, sweet sesame-ginger dressing and topped with crunchy sliced almonds. For a complete meal, top with pan-seared chicken or tofu, or serve alongside seared salmon.

8-ounce package shredded cabbage and carrot blend
1 cup roughly chopped fresh cilantro
2 scallions, thinly sliced
½ cup Sesame-Ginger Dressing (page 195) or store bought
¼ cup thinly sliced almonds or slivered almonds

1   In a large mixing bowl, toss the shredded cabbage mixture, cilantro, and scallions. Drizzle with the sesame-ginger dressing, tossing gently to combine.

2   Divide between the serving plates, and top with the almonds.

Spring Mix Salad with Quinoa and Dried Cranberries

The quinoa adds protein and complex carbohydrates, while pecans bring healthy fats and a touch more protein to this filling vegan salad. It's delicious with sweet dried cranberries and spring mix salad greens, or an equal amount of your favorite chopped lettuce.

1 cup quinoa
Sea salt
1½ cups water
4 cups spring mix salad greens
¼ cup dried cranberries
½ cup pecan pieces
½ cup Balsamic Vinaigrette (page 193)

1 In a large pot, add the quinoa, a pinch of sea salt, and the water. Bring to a simmer over medium heat, cover, reduce the heat to low, and cook for 15 to 20 minutes, or until all the liquid is absorbed. Fluff with a fork, and allow to cool for 10 minutes.

2 In a large mixing bowl, toss the spring mix, cranberries, and pecans. Toss gently with the balsamic vinaigrette to coat. Add the slightly cooled quinoa to the salad, and mix gently.

prep tip: To toast pecans, place the pecans in a dry skillet over medium-high heat for 2 to 3 minutes, shaking regularly, until they are fragrant and toasted.

- VEGAN
- GLUTEN-FREE
- GOOD FOR SHARING

Serves 4

PREP TIME
5 minutes

COOK TIME
20 minutes, plus 10 minutes to cool

PER SERVING (2 CUPS)
Calories: 438
Fat: 27g
Carbs: 46g
Fiber: 6g
Protein: 8g

leftovers tip
Each of the components of this salad can be prepared and stored separately, making it perfect for planning meals in advance. Serve warm or cold.

Watermelon, Tomato, and Feta Salad

- **VEGETARIAN**
- **GLUTEN-FREE**
- **PREP AND SERVE**
- **GOOD FOR SHARING**

Serves 4

PREP TIME
10 minutes

**PER SERVING
(1 CUP)**
Calories: 169
Fat: 12g
Carbs: 11g
Fiber: 1g
Protein: 7g

Sweet watermelon and tomatoes are a delicious contrast to tangy feta cheese in this simple summery salad. It is best when the fruits are fully ripe in season, which is in the late summer. For the best value on feta cheese, buy a whole piece of it, and crumble it yourself; it keeps for up to a month in the refrigerator once opened, giving you plenty of time to plan another meal using it.

2 cups cubed watermelon
2 cups diced tomatoes
½ cup roughly chopped fresh basil
1 tablespoon red wine vinegar
1 tablespoon extra-virgin olive oil
Sea salt
Freshly ground black pepper
4 ounces crumbled feta cheese

1   In a large serving bowl, toss the watermelon, tomatoes, and basil. Drizzle with the red wine vinegar and olive oil. Season with salt and pepper.

2   Add the feta cheese to the salad just before serving.

prep tip
Watermelon and tomatoes taste best when they're served at room temperature. So make the salad shortly before you intend to serve it, or let it come to room temperature before serving.

Caprese Salad

As beautiful and tasty as this classic salad is, it is surprisingly easy. Just assemble and serve. Look for fresh mozzarella cheese near the deli section of the grocery store. It is often stored near the cured meats and other artisan cheeses.

4-ounce ball fresh mozzarella cheese
1 large heirloom tomato, cored
1 tablespoon balsamic vinegar
1 teaspoon extra-virgin olive oil
8 fresh basil leaves, thinly sliced
Sea salt
Freshly ground black pepper

1. Slice the mozzarella cheese and tomato into ¼-inch-thick slices.

2. Stack the cheese and tomato slices in alternating layers on two individual serving plates.

3. Drizzle each with the balsamic vinegar and olive oil, and top with fresh basil. Season with salt and pepper.

■ VEGETARIAN
■ GLUTEN-FREE
■ PREP AND SERVE

Serves 2

PREP TIME
5 minutes

PER SERVING
(¾ CUP)
Calories: 188
Fat: 12g
Carbs: 7g
Fiber: 1g
Protein: 15g

prep tip
To make a basil chiffonade, stack the basil leaves on top of each other and roll into a tight cylinder. Use a sharp chef's knife to make perpendicular cuts, producing small curls of basil.

Classic Grilled Cheese

Serves 1

PREP TIME
5 minutes

COOK TIME
5 minutes

**PER SERVING
(1 SANDWICH)**
Calories: 355
Fat: 18g
Carbs: 38g
Fiber: 6g
Protein: 18g

Want the convenience of a sandwich and the comfort of a warm, home-cooked meal? Look no further than the grilled cheese sandwich. It has all the things you loved about grilled cheese as a kid—the creamy, stretchy cheese center sandwiched between crispy, buttery slices of bread; though this can be made with a few variations for a more sophisticated palate.

¼ tablespoon butter, at room temperature
2 slices whole-grain bread
1 slice Cheddar cheese
1 slice American cheese

1 Preheat a large skillet over medium heat.

2 Butter 2 slices of bread, and place 1 slice butter-side down in the pan. Add the cheese, and top with the additional buttered bread slice, butter-side up.

3 Cook for 2 to 3 minutes, until the cheese begins to melt and the bottom is golden brown.

4 Flip and cook for another 2 minutes. Slice in half and transfer to a serving plate.

VARIATIONS

Spicy Bacon Grilled Cheese: Make the sandwich according to the provided instructions, using 2 slices of cooked bacon and 2 slices of pepper Jack cheese.

Pizza Margherita Grilled Cheese: Make the sandwich according to the provided instructions, using 2 slices of mozzarella cheese, 4 fresh basil leaves, and 2 slices of fresh tomato.

Prosciutto, Provolone, and Pear Grilled Cheese: Make the sandwich according to the provided instructions, using 2 slices of prosciutto, 2 slices of provolone, and 2 thin slices of pear.

foodie 101
Experiment with new cheeses in your sandwich. Some other great options to try include fontina, Gruyère, provolone, and Parmesan.

prep tip
Make sure the skillet is warmed before you place the sandwich in it. The sandwich will get a nice golden brown crust and cook more quickly than if it is placed in a cold skillet.

Green Bean and Apple Salad with Almonds

Serves 4

PREP TIME
10 minutes

COOK TIME
2 to 3 minutes

PER SERVING
(¾ CUP)
Calories: 182
Fat: 12g
Carbs: 19g
Fiber: 5g
Protein: 4g

insanely easy
Purchase a bag of microwavable green beans. Microwave for about 75 percent of the time suggested on the package. Plunge into ice water, drain, and proceed with the recipe.

Blanching and shocking is a method of preparing vegetables that produces a tender snap. It's good for preparing vegetables for a platter, for later sautéing, or for adding to salads. Blanched vegetables are great to keep on hand for quick dinner prep or a healthy snack.

1 pound green beans, stems removed
1 shallot, minced
Zest and juice of 1 lemon
2 tablespoons extra-virgin olive oil
Sea salt
Freshly ground black pepper
1 Pink Lady or Braeburn apple, cored and thinly sliced
¼ cup roughly chopped roasted almonds

1 Bring a large pot of salted water to a boil over high heat. Prepare a separate bowl full of ice water.

2 Add the green beans to the boiling water, and cook for 2 to 3 minutes, until they're nearly tender but still bright green. Immediately, transfer the beans to the ice water to stop the cooking process. When the beans are cool, drain.

3 In a large measuring cup, combine the shallot, lemon zest and juice, and olive oil. Whisk vigorously. Season with salt and pepper.

4 Arrange the green beans and apples on a serving plate, and drizzle with the dressing. Top with the roasted almonds.

Salmon Sliders with Avocado

When you have all the ingredients on hand, these adorable little sandwiches come together in minutes. You can also replace the smoked salmon with smoked turkey purchased from the deli counter.

- **4 dinner rolls or small hamburger buns**
- **2 tablespoons mayonnaise**
- **4 ounces smoked salmon**
- **1 avocado, cut into thin slices**
- **1 cup arugula**

Slice the rolls in half, and spread lightly with the mayonnaise. Place a few pieces of smoked salmon on the bottom half of each roll. Top with the avocado, arugula, and the remaining half of each roll.

PREP AND SERVE

Serves 2

PREP TIME
5 minutes

**PER SERVING
(2 SLIDERS)**
Calories: 512
Fat: 32g
Carbs: 40g
Fiber: 8g
Protein: 19g

foodie 101
Arugula is a slightly bitter green with a peppery bite. It is also delicious in salads and should be handled carefully because it bruises easily.

Greek Pita Sandwich

- VEGETARIAN
  OPTION
- PREP AND SERVE

Serves 4

PREP TIME
5 minutes

**PER SERVING
(2 PITA HALVES WITH
1 CUP FILLING)**
Calories: 511
Fat: 24g
Carbs: 41g
Fiber: 3g
Protein: 34g

prep tip
Purchase cooked
chicken at the deli
counter, or buy a
rotisserie chicken
and use it to make
meals throughout
the week.

Pita bread is naturally hollow, and the space inside is perfect for filling
with savory ingredients. This sandwich is packed with flavor from
briny Kalamata olives, sweet plum tomatoes, and crunchy cucumber.

¼ cup pitted Kalamata olives, halved
1 cup diced plum tomatoes
1 cup diced cucumber
2 cups sliced or diced cooked chicken
2 teaspoons extra-virgin olive oil
1 teaspoon red wine vinegar
Sea salt
Freshly ground black pepper
4 pita breads, halved

1 In a medium mixing bowl, combine the olives, tomatoes, cucumber,
   and chicken. Drizzle with the olive oil and red wine vinegar, and
   season with salt and pepper.

2 Divide the mixture between the pita halves, and serve.

VARIATION

Vegetarian Greek Pita Sandwich: Swap the chicken for 1½ cups
of rinsed, drained chickpeas (from 1 can) and ½ cup of crumbled
feta cheese.

Essential Tuna Salad Sandwich

Tuna salad is inexpensive, easy to make, and filled with the protein, fat, and complex carbs to keep you energized all afternoon.

1 (6-ounce) can water-packed tuna

1 celery stalk, finely diced

3 tablespoons mayonnaise

Freshly ground black pepper

2 lettuce leaves

2 slices whole-grain bread

1 In a small mixing bowl, combine the tuna, celery, and mayonnaise. Season with pepper.

2 Place the mixture on 1 slice of bread, and top with the lettuce leaves.

3 Add the remaining slice of bread to make a sandwich, and serve.

VARIATIONS

Tuna-Stuffed Avocado: Prepare the tuna, celery, and mayonnaise as directed. Divide the mixture between two avocado halves, and serve.

Tuna Melt: Prepare the tuna, celery, and mayonnaise as directed. Place the mixture on 1 slice of bread, omit the lettuce, and add 2 slices of Cheddar cheese. Heat a large skillet over medium heat. Coat the outside of the sandwich in 1 tablespoon of soft butter. Fry for 3 to 4 minutes on each side, or until the cheese is melted.

■ **PREP AND SERVE**

Serves 1

PREP TIME
5 minutes

**PER SERVING
(1 SANDWICH)**
Calories: 697
Fat: 39g
Carbs: 39g
Fiber: 7g
Protein: 51g

prep tip
To keep the bread from getting soggy, store the tuna salad and bread separately until you're ready to eat the sandwich.

Roasted Red Pepper and Provolone Sandwich

▪ VEGETARIAN
▪ PREP AND SERVE

Serves 2

PREP TIME
5 minutes

**PER SERVING
(1 SANDWICH)**
Calories: 473
Fat: 33g
Carbs: 24g
Fiber: 2g
Protein: 20g

This savory vegetarian sandwich is perfect for picnics or long hikes. Wrap it tightly in plastic until you're ready to serve.

1 loaf herbed focaccia bread, halved horizontally

2 tablespoons extra-virgin olive oil

2 jarred roasted red peppers, sliced in wide strips

4 ounces provolone cheese, sliced

1 cup arugula or roughly chopped spinach

Sea salt

Freshly ground black pepper

Brush the cut-side of the focaccia with olive oil. Top one half with red peppers and then with the cheese and arugula. Season with salt and pepper. Close with the remaining slice of focaccia. Slice the large sandwich in half to make 2 servings.

prep tip: To make your own roasted red peppers, cut a pepper in half, and remove its core. Coat the skin with a thin layer of canola oil, and place the halves skin-side up on a broiler pan. Broil for 10 minutes, or until the skin is charred. Carefully transfer the peppers to a covered container, and let them steam for 10 minutes. Remove the charred peel. Use the peppers immediately, or refrigerate until you're ready to use.

Chicken Salad Wrap

Chicken salad is one of my favorite ways to use up leftover cooked chicken. I love the creamy, tangy mayonnaise, sweet dried cranberries, and crunchy celery. While this wrap is a healthy meal on its own, you can add easily sneak in some lettuce to get your green fix.

2 cups diced cooked chicken
1 stalk celery, diced
¼ cup dried cranberries
¼ cup mayonnaise
Sea salt
Freshly ground black pepper
2 flour tortillas

OPTIONAL ADD-INS
1 cup shredded lettuce

1 In a small mixing bowl, combine the chicken, celery, cranberries, and mayonnaise. Season with salt and pepper.

2 Divide the mixture between the two tortillas, placing it in the center of each. Add the shredded lettuce (if using). Fold one side of the tortilla over the filling, fold in each end, and roll the tortilla as if making a burrito.

■ PREP AND SERVE

Serves 2

PREP TIME
5 minutes

PER SERVING
(1 WRAP)
Calories: 567
Fat: 28g
Carbs: 49g
Fiber: 2g
Protein: 32g

leftovers tip
The chicken salad can also be used to fill lettuce cups or as a topping for salad.

Vegetable Wrap with Hummus

■ VEGAN
■ PREP AND SERVE

Serves 2

PREP TIME
5 minutes

PER SERVING
(1 WRAP)
Calories: 726
Fat: 38g
Carbs: 81g
Fiber: 15g
Protein: 22g

This wrap is loaded with colorful vegetables and tangy hummus. The spread is a good source of protein and healthy fats, making it a great option for vegetarians and vegans. You can make your own Hummus (page 189) or purchase it from the deli section of the grocery store.

1 cup Hummus (page 189) or store bought
2 large flour tortillas
1 small zucchini, halved crosswise and sliced in spears
1 red bell pepper, cored and thinly sliced
2 cups roughly chopped spinach
Sea salt
Freshly ground black pepper

1 Spread ½ cup of the hummus over the center of each tortilla. Place the zucchini, bell pepper, and spinach over the hummus, keeping the vegetables in the center of the tortilla. Season with salt and pepper.

2 Fold one side of the tortilla over the filling, fold in each end, and roll the tortilla as if making a burrito.

ingredient tip
Use sun-dried tomato or spinach tortillas for added flavor.

Baked Veggie Quesadilla

This easy vegetarian entrée is perfect for weeknight dinners or a quick snack. It also makes a good game-day appetizer and is a welcome addition to the buffet, especially for vegetarians, who are usually relegated to vegetable platters and chips. Whip up a batch of 5-Minute Guacamole (page 188) to serve alongside the quesadillas for an even more filling meal.

4 large flour tortillas
½ cup refried beans
½ cup thinly sliced mushrooms
¼ cup thinly sliced red onion
1 cup shredded Mexican cheese blend

1 Preheat the oven to 350°F.

2 Place 2 tortillas on a baking sheet. Spread ¼ cup of the refried beans onto each tortilla, and top with ¼ cup of mushrooms, 2 tablespoons of red onion, and ½ cup of cheese. Top each with 1 of the remaining tortillas.

3 Bake for 12 to 15 minutes, or until the tortillas are crisp and the cheese is melted.

4 Slice the quesadillas into wedges, and serve.

■ **VEGETARIAN**
■ **MICROWAVE FRIENDLY**
■ **GOOD FOR SHARING**

Serves 2

PREP TIME
5 minutes

COOK TIME
12 to 15 minutes

PER SERVING (1 QUESADILLA)
Calories: 694
Fat: 29g
Carbs: 80g
Fiber: 7g
Protein: 28g

prep tip
You can also prepare these quesadillas in the microwave. Place each quesadilla on a microwave-safe plate. Cook individually on high for 1 minute, flip over, and cook on high for another 30 seconds, or until the cheese is melted.

Basic Burger

■ GOOD FOR
SHARING

Serves 4

PREP TIME
5 minutes

COOK TIME
15 minutes

PER SERVING
(1 BURGER)
Calories: 441
Fat: 24g
Carbs: 30g
Fiber: 2g
Protein: 25g

Gourmet burger joints are huge in California where I live, but as far as I'm concerned, perfectly seared ground beef, a juicy tomato slice, shredded lettuce, and spicy red onion slices need no improvement. Don't mess with perfection! Here are the basics of how to prepare a burger, and a few of my favorite add-ins. The recipe doesn't call for ketchup, mustard, or mayonnaise, because individual preferences tend to vary so much, but use whichever ones you like to top your burger.

16 ounces ground beef
Sea salt
Freshly ground black pepper
4 hamburger buns, toasted
1 large tomato, thinly sliced
4 lettuce leaves, thinly sliced
½ red onion, thinly sliced

OPTIONAL ADD-INS
Cooked bacon
Caramelized onions
Sliced avocado
Dill pickles
Sliced Cheddar cheese

1 Preheat a large skillet over medium heat until hot, about 2 minutes.

2 Form the ground beef into 4 patties, flattening them with the palm of your hand so they are thinner in the center and slightly wider in diameter than the buns; they will shrink during cooking. Season generously with salt and pepper.

3 Sear the burger patties in the hot skillet for about 3 to 4 minutes on each side for medium-rare. They should be deeply browned on the exterior and hot throughout, but still slightly pink in the center.

4 Serve the burgers on toasted buns with the tomato, lettuce, and onion, as well as condiments and any add-ins (if using).

cooking tip
Do not press down on the burgers during cooking, or you will cause them to release all of their flavorful juices.

ingredient tip
Ground beef with a ratio of 85 percent lean to 15 percent fat works well for making hamburgers.

GAZPACHO (PAGE 104)

Chapter 5

SOUPS AND STEWS

Ramen

■ VEGAN OPTION
■ MICROWAVE FRIENDLY
■ GOOD FOR SHARING

Serves 1

PREP TIME
5 minutes

COOK TIME
5 minutes

PER SERVING
(1 BOWL RAMEN)
Calories: 282
Fat: 10g
Carbs: 23g
Fiber: 2g
Protein: 27g

No college cookbook would be complete without a tribute to the inexpensive noodle dish that has fueled an infinite number of late-night study sessions and hurried lunches between midday classes. This version relies on the packaged noodles but swaps the chemical-laden sauce packet for healthier chicken or vegetable broth. The recipe includes three variations inspired by the original Japanese recipes for ramen noodles.

2 cups chicken or vegetable broth
1 (3-ounce) package ramen noodles
1 green onion, thinly sliced
2 button mushrooms, thinly sliced
1 tablespoon soy sauce
Sea salt
Freshly ground black pepper

1 In a small pot, bring the broth to a simmer. Add the ramen noodles, and cook for 3 minutes.

2 Stir in the green onion, mushrooms, and soy sauce. Season with salt and pepper. Serve immediately.

VARIATIONS

Ramen with Soft-Boiled Egg: Prepare according to the recipe. Top the ramen with 1 soft-boiled egg (see page 49), halved, just before serving.

Miso Ramen: Omit the mushrooms and soy sauce, and stir in ½ cup of frozen peas, corn, and carrots just before serving. Remove ½ cup of soup from the pot, and mix together with 1 tablespoon of red or white miso until combined. Add the soup back to the pot, and mix.

Thai Chicken Ramen: Heat the broth, and stir in ½ cup of shredded cooked chicken in the last minute of cooking. Mix in 1 teaspoon of red curry paste and ¼ cup of coconut milk, and top with a handful of bean sprouts and serve.

prep tip
To prepare this dish in the microwave, heat the broth in a microwave-safe dish on high for 2 minutes. Stir in the ramen noodles, and microwave on high for another 3 to 5 minutes, or until the noodles are soft.

Roasted Red Pepper and Tomato Soup

- VEGAN
- GLUTEN-FREE

Serves 2 to 4

PREP TIME
10 minutes

COOK TIME
10 minutes

PER SERVING
(2 CUPS)
Calories: 95
Fat: 3g
Carbs: 15g
Fiber: 4g
Protein: 3g

Roasting vegetables—especially tomatoes and peppers—brings out their natural sweetness and adds complexity. Although you can purchase roasted peppers in a jar, the flavor of freshly roasted peppers is far superior. Bonus: Unlike most things you might put under the broiler, you want to burn the peppers!

2 cups grape or cherry tomatoes
Extra-virgin olive oil
2 red bell peppers, cored, halved, and seeded
Sea salt
Freshly ground black pepper
2 cups vegetable broth, warmed
2 tablespoons apple cider vinegar
1 teaspoon smoked paprika

1 Preheat the broiler, and place the oven rack on the top level.

2 In a large mixing bowl, toss the tomatoes with a drizzle of olive oil, and spread out on half of a broiler pan.

3 Brush the bell peppers with olive oil, and place skin-side up on the other half of the pan.

prep tip
For a perfectly smooth soup, pour it through a fine-mesh sieve.

4 Place the pan under the broiler, and roast until the tomatoes are split and the peppers are charred, about 5 minutes. Carefully transfer the peppers to a separate container, season with salt and pepper, and cover tightly. Allow to steam for 5 minutes, and then carefully remove the charred skins and discard.

5 Put the tomatoes and peeled peppers into a blender, and add the vegetable broth, vinegar, and paprika. Purée until smooth. Divide among the bowls.

VARIATION

Tomato-Basil Soup: Combine 1 (28-ounce) can of puréed plum tomatoes, ¼ cup of olive oil, 1 cup of vegetable broth, ½ cup of shredded fresh basil, and ½ teaspoon of sea salt in a small pot. Bring to a simmer.

Chicken Soup

■ GLUTEN-FREE
■ GOOD FOR
  SHARING

Serves 2

PREP TIME
5 minutes

COOK TIME
10 minutes

**PER SERVING
(2 CUPS)**
Calories: 387
Fat: 17g
Carbs: 8g
Fiber: 1g
Protein: 51g

prep tip
If you're using egg
noodles, stir the noo-
dles in after adding
the broth. Cook for
8 minutes, and then
add the chicken.

On a cold rainy day, is there anything more comforting than chicken soup? I can't think of anything. When you have all of the ingredients on hand, this version comes together quickly. Serve with a hunk of crusty bread or whole-grain toast.

1 tablespoon canola oil
1 carrot, diced
1 celery stalk, diced
2 garlic cloves, minced
4 cups chicken broth
2 cups shredded cooked chicken
Sea salt
Freshly ground black pepper

OPTIONAL ADD-IN
1 cup egg noodles

1 In a small pot, heat the oil over medium heat. Cook the carrot and celery for 3 to 5 minutes, until they begin to soften. Add the garlic, and cook for another 30 seconds, until fragrant.

2 Pour in the chicken broth, and bring to a simmer. Stir in the cooked chicken, and cook for another 2 minutes, or until the chicken is heated through and the vegetables are tender. Season with salt and pepper.

Tortellini Soup

This delicious and filling vegetarian soup is so easy to prepare and tastes like something your grandmother would have made. It makes canned soup question its very existence. The recipe calls for a lot of olive oil, and you can cut down on it if you wish, but it does give the soup body.

¼ cup extra-virgin olive oil
1 yellow onion, diced
Sea salt
4 garlic cloves, smashed
1 (15-ounce) can whole plum tomatoes, hand crushed
4 cups vegetable broth
1 (16-ounce) package cheese-filled spinach tortellini
Freshly ground black pepper

1 In a large pot, heat the olive oil over medium heat. Cook the onion with a pinch of salt until softened, about 10 minutes.

2 Add the garlic, and cook for 1 minute.

3 Add the plum tomatoes and vegetable broth, and bring to a simmer.

4 Add the tortellini to the soup, and simmer according to the package instructions, or until cooked through. Season with pepper.

■ VEGETARIAN

Serves 4

PREP TIME
5 minutes

COOK TIME
30 minutes

**PER SERVING
(1½ CUPS)**
Calories: 401
Fat: 21g
Carbs: 44g
Fiber: 2g
Protein: 13g

insanely easy
Although whole plum tomatoes are more flavorful than canned diced tomatoes, purchase the latter if you want to cut down on prep time.

Chorizo and Kidney Bean Chili

■ GLUTEN-FREE
■ GOOD FOR
  SHARING

Serves 4

PREP TIME
5 minutes

COOK TIME
20 minutes

**PER SERVING
(1½ CUPS)**
Calories: 752
Fat: 48g
Carbs: 39g
Fiber: 13g
Protein: 40g

foodie 101
Chili powder is a
mixture of spices,
namely ground
dried chiles. It also
includes cumin,
garlic, and oregano,
along with other
spices.

Most chili begins with ground beef or sliced steak, but this version gets a generous dose of flavor from chorizo, which is made with ground pork and smoked paprika. This chili is perfect on its own or paired with warmed corn tortillas and a dollop of sour cream.

1 tablespoon canola oil
16 ounces chorizo, casings removed
1 large red onion, diced
2 (15-ounce) cans fire-roasted tomatoes
2 (15-ounce) cans kidney beans, drained
2 tablespoons chili powder
Sea salt
Freshly ground black pepper

1 In a large pot, heat the oil over medium-high heat. Sauté the chorizo in the oil until browned, about 5 minutes. Transfer to a bowl.

2 Add the onion to the pot, and cook until barely softened, about 5 minutes.

3 Add the tomatoes, scraping up the browned bits from the bottom of the pan. Stir in the kidney beans, chili powder, and cooked chorizo. Season with salt and pepper.

4 Cook for 10 minutes to allow the flavors to come together.

Chipotle Black Bean Chili

The smoky, spicy flavor of chipotle peppers in adobo sauce takes this vegan chili to another level. For a less intense heat, scrape the seeds from the peppers before mincing them and folding them into the chili. Cool things off with a little sour cream or sliced avocado and corn chips for serving.

2 tablespoons canola oil
1 red onion, diced
4 garlic cloves, smashed
¼ cup minced chipotle peppers in adobo
2 (15-ounce) cans black beans, drained
1 (15-ounce) can fire-roasted tomatoes
Sea salt
Freshly ground black pepper

1 In a large pot, heat the oil over medium heat. Cook the onion and garlic until soft, about 10 minutes.

2 Add the chipotle peppers, black beans, and tomatoes, and bring to a simmer. Season with salt and pepper. Cook for an additional 10 minutes.

3 Serve with avocado or sour cream and corn chips.

■ **VEGAN**
■ **GLUTEN-FREE**

Serves 4

PREP TIME
5 minutes

COOK TIME
20 minutes

**PER SERVING
(1¼ CUPS)**
Calories: 289
Fat: 8g
Carbs: 43g
Fiber: 17g
Protein: 15g

prep tip
For an extra-creamy chili, remove 1½ cups of the cooked chili, and purée in a blender until smooth. Return to the pot and stir.

Gazpacho

■ VEGAN
■ GLUTEN-FREE
■ PREP AND SERVE

Serves 4

PREP TIME
5 minutes

PER SERVING
(1 CUP)
Calories: 94
Fat: 7g
Carbs: 7g
Fiber: 2g
Protein: 2g

leftovers tip
Leftovers can be
stored for up to 1 day
in the refrigerator.
However, if you plan
to have extras, leave
the shallots out
until you're ready
to serve. Otherwise,
they can easily over-
power the soup.

This refreshing Spanish soup is served cold. It is perfect for
late-summer barbecues at the start of each school year. That's
when tomatoes are still in season, and if you're lucky, the weather
is still warm.

1 pound fresh tomatoes, cored and diced
1 hothouse cucumber, peeled, seeded, and diced
2 tablespoons red wine vinegar
2 tablespoons extra-virgin olive oil
Sea salt
Freshly ground black pepper
2 shallots, minced
4 fresh basil leaves, minced

OPTIONAL ADD-INS
1 cup diced mango
1 cup diced red bell pepper

1 In a blender jar, add half of the tomatoes and half of the cucumber
along with the vinegar and olive oil. Purée until smooth. Season
with salt and pepper.

2 Stir in the remaining tomatoes and cucumber, and the shallots and
basil. Serve immediately, or chill until ready to serve.

Tortilla Soup

This was a family favorite at my house and one that I looked forward to when I visited my parents during school breaks. While the more typical version of this soup uses corn tortilla strips, this version uses tortilla chips to cut down on the prep time.

■ **GLUTEN-FREE**
■ **GOOD FOR SHARING**

Serves 4

PREP TIME
5 minutes

COOK TIME
15 minutes

PER SERVING (1½ CUPS SOUP WITH 20 TORTILLA CHIPS)
Calories: 649
Fat: 43g
Carbs: 43g
Fiber: 4g
Protein: 25g

2 tablespoons canola oil
1 pound ground beef
Sea salt
Freshly ground black pepper
1 cup diced yellow onion
1 (15-ounce) can fire-roasted tomatoes with chiles
1 tablespoon chili powder
2 cups water
8 cups tortilla chips

OPTIONAL ADD-IN
1 cup shredded Cheddar cheese

1 In a large pot, heat the oil over high heat. Season the ground beef with salt and pepper, and cook until browned, about 5 minutes. Transfer the beef to a separate dish.

2 Lower the heat to medium. Cook the onion in the same pot until it begins to soften, about 5 minutes.

3 Add the tomatoes, chili powder, and the water, and bring to a simmer. Return the beef to the pan, and cook for another 5 minutes. Serve with the tortilla chips and shredded cheese (if using).

leftovers tip
This soup is even better the next day when the flavors have come together better. Store in a covered container for up to 3 days, and reheat before serving.

Broccoli-Cheddar Soup

■ **VEGETARIAN**
■ **GLUTEN-FREE**

Serves 4

PREP TIME
5 minutes

COOK TIME
10 to 12 minutes

PER SERVING
(1¾ CUPS)
Calories: 343
Fat: 26g
Carbs: 13g
Fiber: 2g
Protein: 19g

prep tip
When adding cheese to a soup or sauce, it should be 150°F or less, about the temperature of a latte, to prevent the cheese from curdling.

Broccoli-cheese soup is a one-pot vegetarian meal that is easy to pull together. I love the pronounced flavor of sharp Cheddar cheese, but use whatever shredded cheese you have on hand. Serve with a slice of crusty bread and a glass of cold apple cider for a quintessential fall meal.

1 head broccoli, broken into florets
2 garlic cloves, minced
4 cups vegetable or chicken broth
1 cup heavy cream
2 cups shredded sharp Cheddar cheese
Sea salt
Freshly ground black pepper

1. In a large pot, add the broccoli, garlic, and vegetable broth, and bring to a simmer over medium heat. Cook for 7 minutes, or until the broccoli is barely tender and still bright green.

2. Stir in the heavy cream, and cook for 2 to 3 minutes. Remove the pot from the heat, and allow to cool for 1 to 2 minutes. Stir in the Cheddar cheese. Continue stirring until melted. Season the soup with salt and pepper.

ingredient tip: To save time, use one package of frozen broccoli florets and cook until just heated through, about 2 minutes.

Curried Lentil Soup

Lentils are a great source of protein and complex carbohydrates in this flavorful vegan soup. It can easily be doubled to share with friends. For even more protein, serve with a generous scoop of plain yogurt.

2 tablespoons canola oil
1 yellow onion, diced
Sea salt
1 cup green lentils, rinsed and sorted
4 cups vegetable broth
2 tablespoons tomato paste
1 tablespoon curry powder
Freshly ground black pepper

1 In a large pot, heat the canola oil over medium heat. Cook the onion with a pinch of sea salt for 2 to 3 minutes, until it begins to soften.

2 Add the lentils, broth, tomato paste, and curry powder, and bring to a simmer.

3 Cover and cook on low for 20 minutes. Season with salt and pepper.

ingredient tip: Purchase tomato paste in a tube so you can use just what you need. Alternatively, use 1 tablespoon of ketchup.

■ VEGAN
■ GLUTEN-FREE
■ GOOD FOR SHARING

Serves 2 to 4

PREP TIME
5 minutes

COOK TIME
25 minutes

PER SERVING
(1 CUP)
Calories: 258
Fat: 8g
Carbs: 35g
Fiber: 15g
Protein: 14g

prep tip
When you rinse and sort the lentils, keep an eye out for small pebbles or sticks. Occasionally they end up in dried legumes.

Corn Chowder

■ VEGAN
■ GLUTEN-FREE

Serves 2 to 4

PREP TIME
5 minutes

COOK TIME
20 minutes

PER SERVING
(1½ CUPS)
Calories: 507
Fat: 21g
Carbs: 78g
Fiber: 9g
Protein: 14g

prep tip
Take care when
puréeing hot soups.
Lift the blender lid
once or twice when
the motor is not run-
ning to allow steam
to escape.

I love this sweet, creamy corn chowder. It is thickened with a diced potato and with a purée of some of the soup. To make a complete meal, serve it with tortilla chips and 5-Minute Guacamole (page 188).

2 tablespoons canola oil
1 small yellow onion, minced
4 cups corn kernels, fresh, or frozen and defrosted
1 small russet potato, peeled and diced
2 cups vegetable broth
2 cups unsweetened nondairy milk, such as almond milk
Sea salt
Freshly ground black pepper

OPTIONAL ADD-INS
Thinly sliced scallions
Shredded Cheddar cheese
Crumbled bacon

1 In a large pot, heat the oil over medium heat. Cook the onion for 5 minutes, until slightly softened.

2 Add the corn, potato, broth, and nondairy milk, and bring to a gentle simmer. Cook for 15 minutes, until the potato is soft.

3 Carefully transfer 2 cups of the soup to a blender and purée until completely smooth. Cover the top of the blender lid with a kitchen towel to prevent any splatters.

4 Return the puréed soup to the pot, and stir it into the soup. Season with salt and pepper, and serve with any add-ins (if using).

Mushroom Barley Soup

Barley is a good source of plant-based protein. It is often paired with beef in the classic beef barley soup. This version uses mushrooms, which are surprisingly filling and flavorful and make the soup virtually fat-free.

1 yellow onion, diced
4 garlic cloves, minced
2 cups thinly sliced cremini mushrooms
¾ cup pearl barley
4 cups vegetable broth
Sea salt
Freshly ground black pepper

1 Place the onion, garlic, mushrooms, barley, and vegetable broth in a large pot, and bring to a simmer. Season with salt and pepper.

2 Cover and cook for 25 minutes, or until the barley is tender.

■ VEGAN
■ GOOD FOR SHARING

Serves 4

PREP TIME
5 minutes

COOK TIME
25 minutes

PER SERVING (1 CUP)
Calories: 166
Fat: 1g
Carbs: 36g
Fiber: 7g
Protein: 6g

foodie 101
Cremini mushrooms, also called "baby bellas," are smaller versions of the meaty portobello mushrooms. You can also use button mushrooms.

PASTA PUTTANESCA
(PAGE 115)

Chapter 6

VEGE-TARIAN AND VEGAN MAINS

Spaghetti Marinara

Serves 4

PREP TIME
10 minutes

COOK TIME
20 minutes

PER SERVING
(1 CUP)
Calories: 343
Fat: 12g
Carbs: 55g
Fiber: 5g
Protein: 9g

Marinara sauce was one of the first savory recipes I tried to make while I was still living at home. Only one tiny little problem—although I had eaten spaghetti for my entire life, I really had no idea what went into the sauce beyond tomatoes. I blundered my way through that first attempt and eventually consulted a cookbook before mastering the essential sauce.

3 tablespoons extra-virgin olive oil
1 yellow onion, minced
4 garlic cloves, minced
1 (15-ounce) can tomato sauce
1 (15-ounce) can plum tomatoes, hand crushed
Sea salt
Freshly ground black pepper
1 (8-ounce) package spaghetti noodles

OPTIONAL ADD-INS
Fresh basil, stems removed and chopped
Grated Parmesan cheese

1 In a large pot, heat the olive oil over medium heat. Cook the onion for 5 to 7 minutes, until it is soft and golden.

2 Add the garlic, and cook for 1 minute. Add the tomato sauce and plum tomatoes. Season with salt and pepper. Simmer uncovered for 5 minutes.

3 Bring a large pot of salted water to a boil over high heat. Add the dry spaghetti noodles, and stir to separate. Reduce the heat to medium, and cook uncovered for 7 to 9 minutes until the noodles are still slightly chewy. Drain thoroughly. Transfer the pasta to the marinara sauce and toss gently to coat the noodles in sauce. Top with any add-ins (if using), and serve.

foodie 101
Pasta should be cooked "al dente," which means "to the tooth" in Italian. That is, it should be slightly chewy when you bite into it.

VARIATIONS

Zucchini Noodle Spaghetti: Prepare the sauce as directed in steps 1 and 2 on the previous page. Use 2 medium zucchini to make noodles with a spiralizer tool or a vegetable peeler. Sprinkle a little bit of salt on the noodles, then wrap them in a paper towel and let them sit for about 10 minutes to draw out water. Add the zucchini noodles to the sauce, and cook until just heated through.

Roasted Spaghetti Squash: Preheat the oven to 400°F. Cut a spaghetti squash into 1-inch-thick circles. Scoop the strings and seeds from the center of each round. Place the squash circles on a rimmed baking sheet with ¼ cup of water. Bake for 25 minutes. Prepare the sauce as directed in steps 1 and 2. Using a fork, carefully scrape the thin strands from each piece of spaghetti squash to make long, thin noodles. Top with the sauce.

Spaghetti with Mushrooms and Herbs: Prepare the spaghetti noodles as directed in step 3. Heat 1 tablespoon of butter in a skillet over medium-high heat, and cook 2 cups of sliced mushrooms until browned, about 5 minutes. Add 1 teaspoon of minced fresh thyme and 2 minced garlic cloves, and cook about 30 seconds. Add the cooked pasta to the skillet and season with salt and pepper.

Macaroni and Cheese

■ VEGETARIAN

Serves 4

PREP TIME
5 minutes

COOK TIME
15 minutes

**PER SERVING
(1 CUP)**
Calories: 500
Fat: 26g
Carbs: 48g
Fiber: 2g
Protein: 23g

foodie 101
Béchamel is a basic white sauce made with flour, fat (usually butter), and milk. It forms the basis of many creamy dishes, and learning to make a good béchamel is essential to your culinary repertoire.

This slightly grown-up version of the childhood staple involves no packages of neon powdered cheese. Instead, sharp Cheddar cheese stands up to the creamy béchamel sauce, yielding a flavorful vegetarian entrée. It is still receptive to all the add-ins you may enjoy—especially hot dogs and peas.

1 (8-ounce) package elbow macaroni noodles
Sea salt
2 tablespoons all-purpose flour
2 tablespoons butter
1 cup 2 percent milk
2 cups shredded sharp Cheddar cheese
Freshly ground black pepper

1 Bring a large pot of salted water to a boil over medium heat. Cook the macaroni noodles according to the package directions, about 7 to 10 minutes, or until al dente. Drain well using a colander.

2 While the pasta drains, add the flour and butter to the pot, and cook until thick and bubbling, about 1 minute. Add the milk to the pot, and whisk vigorously to break up any lumps.

3 Reduce the heat to low, and cook the sauce until it thickens, about 2 minutes. Do not boil the sauce.

4 Remove the pot from the heat, and stir in the cheese. Continue stirring until all the cheese is melted, about 1 to 2 minutes.

5 Fold in the macaroni noodles, season with salt and pepper, and serve.

Pasta Puttanesca

Liven up basic pasta with the brininess of capers and olives in this dish with a classic sauce. If you have red pepper flakes in your pantry, use that in place of black pepper for more heat and complexity. Garnish the finished pasta, if you'd like, with ¼ cup minced fresh parsley, and stir before serving.

1 (8-ounce) package penne pasta
Sea salt
3 tablespoons extra-virgin olive oil
4 garlic cloves, minced
2 tablespoons capers, drained
¼ cup pitted Kalamata olives, roughly chopped
1 (15-ounce) can plum tomatoes, hand crushed
Freshly ground black pepper
¼ cup minced fresh parsley

1 Bring a large pot of salted water to a boil over high heat. Add the penne, and stir to separate. Reduce the heat to medium, and cook uncovered for 7 to 8 minutes, until still slightly chewy. Drain thoroughly.

2 In a large skillet, heat the olive oil over medium heat. Cook the garlic for 1 minute, until fragrant. Add the capers and olives, and cook for another 2 minutes.

3 Add the plum tomatoes. Season with salt and pepper. Simmer uncovered for 2 to 3 minutes.

4 Transfer the pasta to the sauce, and toss gently to coat it in sauce.

▪ VEGAN
▪ GOOD FOR SHARING

Serves 4

PREP TIME
5 minutes

COOK TIME
15 minutes

PER SERVING (1 CUP)
Calories: 329
Fat: 14g
Carbs: 46g
Fiber: 3g
Protein: 8g

foodie 101
Capers are edible flower buds from the caper bush. They are typically pickled, as are caper berries, which are the fruit of the same bush.

Garlicky Cauliflower Linguine

■ VEGAN OPTION
■ GLUTEN-FREE
   OPTION

Serves 4

PREP TIME
5 minutes

COOK TIME
10 minutes

PER SERVING
(1½ CUPS)
Calories: 393
Fat: 16g
Carbs: 59g
Fiber: 6g
Protein: 10g

Cauliflower is an underrated vegetable, but it has a fun texture and mild flavor, making it an excellent addition to a wide variety of cuisines. It pairs especially well with raisins and garlic.

1 (8-ounce) package fettuccine noodles
Sea salt
¼ cup olive oil, plus 2 tablespoons
¼ cup water
1 head cauliflower, broken into small florets
¼ cup raisins
4 garlic cloves, minced
½ cup grated Parmesan cheese (optional)

1 Bring a large pot of salted water to a boil over medium heat. Cook the fettuccine according to the package directions, about 8 to 10 minutes. Drain in a colander.

2 In a skillet, heat ¼ cup of olive oil. Add the cauliflower and cook until it begins to sizzle. Add the water, cover the pan, and cook for 7 minutes.

3 Remove the lid, add the raisins, and cook until almost no liquid remains in the pan, about 2 minutes. Add the garlic and cook for 30 seconds.

4 Transfer the pasta to a serving dish, drizzle with the remaining olive oil, and season with salt and pepper. Top the pasta with the cauliflower mixture, and mix in the Parmesan cheese (if using).

substitution tip
To make this gluten-free, use gluten-free fettuccine. If you cannot find it, you can use any shape of pasta that is available, such as spaghetti or linguine.

Roasted Vegetables with Orzo and Feta

A couple of my closest friends are college professors, and they prepared this delicious dinner using gluten-free orzo. What a delicious surprise, and worthy of all who avoid gluten but love pasta.

4 tablespoons extra-virgin olive oil, divided
4 cups assorted chopped vegetables (zucchini, cherry tomatoes, and/or bell peppers)
Sea salt
Freshly ground black pepper
2 cups gluten-free orzo
Zest and juice of 1 lemon
1 cup roughly chopped fresh basil leaves
8 ounces crumbled feta cheese

1 Preheat the oven to 400°F.

2 Place the vegetables in a large bowl. Add 2 tablespoons of olive oil, and toss to coat. Spread the vegetables on a rimmed baking sheet, and season with salt and pepper. Roast for 25 minutes.

3 While the vegetables cook, bring a large pot of salted water to a boil. Cook the orzo for about 10 minutes, until it is firm but still chewy. Drain in a colander.

4 In a large serving dish, combine the roasted vegetables, cooked orzo, lemon zest, and basil. Drizzle with the lemon juice and remaining olive oil, and toss gently to mix. Sprinkle with the feta cheese.

■ **VEGETARIAN**
■ **GLUTEN-FREE**

Serves 4

PREP TIME
5 minutes

COOK TIME
25 minutes

PER SERVING
(1⅔ CUPS)
Calories: 425
Fat: 27g
Carbs: 34g
Fiber: 6g
Protein: 15g

prep tip
Oven roasting at high heat brings out the sweetness and complexity in ordinary vegetables, giving them a caramelized exterior and soft, succulent interior. Make sure not to cover them or crowd the pan.

Super Cheesy Lasagna

■ VEGETARIAN
■ MICROWAVE
FRIENDLY

Serves 8

PREP TIME
5 minutes

COOK TIME
25 minutes

PER SERVING
(1 PIECE)
Calories: 464
Fat: 27g
Carbs: 36g
Fiber: 3g
Protein: 25g

insanely easy
To make this in the microwave, follow the instructions above, and cover the dish with parchment paper and then a plate. Microwave on high for 15 minutes, or until the lasagna noodles are tender.

I have been making some rendition of this lasagna since I was in college. I can now whip it up in just a few minutes using pantry ingredients and store-bought cheese.

1 tablespoon canola oil
1 (15-ounce) container ricotta cheese
1 (8-ounce) bag shredded Italian cheese blend
1 (32-ounce) jar marinara sauce
8 ounces oven-ready lasagna noodles
2 cups roughly chopped fresh basil leaves

1   Preheat the oven to 425°F. Coat the interior of an 8-by-8-inch baking dish with oil.

2   In a large mixing bowl, combine the ricotta cheese and 1½ cups of the Italian cheese blend.

3   Spread ½ cup of marinara sauce in the baking dish. Lay 3 or 4 lasagna noodles into the dish to cover the bottom of it. Spread another ½ cup of sauce over the noodles.

4   Top with a thick layer of the cheese mixture. Sprinkle with a generous handful of basil leaves.

5   Repeat with the remaining lasagna noodles, sauce, cheese, and basil. Finish with the noodles and sauce, and top with the remaining ½ cup of shredded cheese.

6   Bake uncovered for 25 minutes, or until browned and bubbling. Allow to rest for 10 minutes before serving.

Pizza Margherita

Prepared pizza crusts make dinner a cinch. You can even cook them in the microwave for a quick meal. This classic vegetarian pizza is similar to the traditional cheese pizza but gets extra flavor from fresh mozzarella cheese and thinly sliced basil leaves.

4 (6-inch) pizza crusts
4 tablespoons olive oil
8 ounces fresh mozzarella cheese, thinly sliced
2 ripe tomatoes, thinly sliced
½ cup thinly sliced fresh basil leaves

1 Preheat the oven to 400°F. Place the pizza crusts onto a rimmed baking sheet.

2 Brush the crusts with the olive oil. Top with the mozzarella cheese and tomato slices.

3 Bake for 10 minutes, or until the mozzarella is melted and the tomatoes are wilted.

4 Top with the fresh basil leaves.

VARIATION

Havarti-Mushroom Pizza: Replace the toppings with 4 ounces of sliced Havarti cheese, 1 tablespoon each of minced fresh thyme and rosemary (or ½ teaspoon each of if dried), and 1 cup of thinly sliced mushrooms. For even more flavor, sauté the mushrooms in butter for 5 minutes, until well browned, before adding them to the pizza.

▪ **VEGETARIAN**
▪ **MICROWAVE FRIENDLY**

Serves 4

PREP TIME
5 minutes

COOK TIME
10 minutes

PER SERVING (1 PIZZA)
Calories: 482
Fat: 31g
Carbs: 35g
Fiber: 3g
Protein: 20g

foodie 101
Fresh mozzarella cheese is formed into a ball shape and stored in liquid. It has a soft, delicate texture and a mild, fresh flavor. Look for it alongside shredded mozzarella cheese or in the specialty cheese section of the grocery store.

BRC Bowl

- VEGAN
- GLUTEN-FREE
- MICROWAVE FRIENDLY

Serves 4

PREP TIME
5 minutes

COOK TIME
10 minutes

PER SERVING
(1½ CUPS)
Calories: 359
Fat: 6g
Carbs: 71g
Fiber: 10g
Protein: 11g

prep tip
If it's available, purchase prepared brown rice to make this recipe come together even faster.

Beans, rice, and corn make up the trio at the heart of this satisfying bowl. This is the perfect vegan meal to prepare once and enjoy all week long. It can be served chilled, or warm the rice, corn, and beans before adding the salsa and guacamole. Together, beans, rice, and corn form a complete protein, supplying all the essential amino acids.

2 cups instant brown rice
2 cups water
1 cup frozen fire-roasted corn kernels, defrosted
1 (15-ounce) can black beans, drained
1 cup Fresh Salsa (page 190) or store bought
1 cup 5-Minute Guacamole (page 188) or store bought

1. In a large pot, combine the rice and the water over medium heat. Bring to a boil, cover, and reduce the heat. Simmer for 5 minutes, and remove from the heat. Let sit undisturbed for 5 minutes. Remove the lid, and fluff with a fork.

2. Divide the rice between the serving bowls. Add ¼ cup of corn and ¼ cup of black beans to each.

3. Top each bowl with ¼ cup of salsa and ¼ cup of guacamole.

   ingredient tip: Although any good-quality frozen corn can be used, I recommend Trader Joe's frozen Fire-Roasted Corn for this recipe.

Quinoa Taco Casserole

This scrumptious vegetarian casserole is loaded with flavor from fire-roasted tomatoes, taco seasoning, and sharp Cheddar cheese. It offers protein, complex carbohydrates, and healthy fats for a complete one-dish meal.

1 tablespoon canola oil
1 cup quinoa
1 (15-ounce) can fire-roasted diced tomatoes with green chilies
1 (15-ounce) can black beans, drained
2 tablespoons taco seasoning
2 cups shredded sharp Cheddar cheese

1 Preheat the oven to 350°F. Coat the inside of an 8-by-8-inch baking dish with canola oil.

2 Add the quinoa, tomatoes, black beans, and taco seasoning to the dish. Add 1½ cups water. Stir gently to mix. Cover the baking dish with a lid, or cover tightly with foil.

3 Bake for 20 minutes. Remove the cover, and top the casserole with cheese. Bake for another 5 minutes, or until the cheese is bubbling.

▪ **VEGETARIAN**
▪ **GLUTEN-FREE**

Serves 4

PREP TIME
5 minutes

COOK TIME
20 minutes

**PER SERVING
(1 CUP)**
Calories: 518
Fat: 28g
Carbs: 48g
Fiber: 9g
Protein: 25g

leftovers tip
This casserole also makes a delicious filling for burritos or can be served with scrambled eggs for a savory breakfast.

ingredient tip
A great product to use in this recipe is Muir Glen Organic Diced Tomatoes, Fire Roasted with Medium Green Chilies.

Roasted-Vegetable Chilaquiles

▦ VEGETARIAN
▦ GLUTEN-FREE
▦ MICROWAVE
   FRIENDLY

Serves 2

PREP TIME
5 minutes

COOK TIME
25 minutes

PER SERVING
(1 CHILAQUILE)
Calories: 630
Fat: 43g
Carbs: 42g
Fiber: 6g
Protein: 24g

I first enjoyed chilaquiles at a restaurant devoted to the cuisine of Mexico City. The restaurant offered spicy posole, the best ceviche I've ever had, and chilaquiles verdes made with house-made salsa verde, roasted vegetables, and queso fresco. Each stack was topped with a fried egg and chives. Here's my simplified version that's as close to the original as I can get without making reservations.

4 cups diced assorted vegetables (zucchini, bell peppers, and/or onions)

2 tablespoons canola oil, divided

Sea salt

Freshly ground black pepper

2 eggs

6 tostada shells

4 ounces queso fresco

1 cup roasted-tomato salsa

1. Preheat the oven to 400°F.

2. Spread the vegetables on a rimmed baking sheet, and drizzle with 1 tablespoon of oil. Toss gently to coat. Season with salt and pepper. Roast for 20 to 25 minutes, until tender and beginning to brown.

3. In a large skillet, heat the remaining 1 tablespoon of oil over medium-high heat. Fry the eggs until the whites are set and the yolks are still runny.

4. To serve, top 1 tostada shell with a generous scoop of roasted vegetables, a spoonful of queso fresco, and a drizzle of salsa. Top with a second tostada shell, vegetables, queso fresco, and salsa. Finish with a final tostada shell, a drizzle of salsa, and a fried egg. Repeat with the remaining ingredients to prepare the second serving.

insanely easy
To keep things really simple, skip the roasted vegetables, and make this recipe in the microwave, layering tostada shells, queso fresco, and salsa as instructed above. Microwave on high for 1 minute. Top with a fried egg.

ingredient tip
A great brand of salsa to use in this recipe is Trader Joe's Double Roasted Salsa. You'll have a little left over in the jar, so be sure to grab a bag of tortilla chips for snacking.

Vegan Enchiladas

▪ VEGAN
▪ MICROWAVE
   FRIENDLY

Serves 4

PREP TIME
5 minutes

COOK TIME
20 minutes

PER SERVING
(2 ENCHILADAS)
Calories: 702
Fat: 16g
Carbs: 119g
Fiber: 11g
Protein: 21g

I love traditional refried beans, especially organic varieties loaded with plenty of spices and green chiles. When you're working with just a few ingredients, choose the best quality you can find (and afford), and let their natural flavors shine. If desired, serve the enchiladas with thinly sliced red onions and 5-Minute Guacamole (page 188).

1 (15-ounce) can enchilada sauce, divided
1 (15-ounce) can refried beans with green chiles
2 cups cooked brown rice
1 cup frozen fire-roasted corn kernels, defrosted
8 flour tortillas

1   Preheat the oven to 350°F.

2   Spread ½ cup of enchilada sauce in a baking dish.

3   In a mixing bowl, combine the refried beans, brown rice, and corn.

4   Scoop a generous dollop of the mixture into 1 tortilla, and roll into a cylinder, folding the ends in as you go. Place the tortilla into the baking dish, seam-side down. Repeat with the remaining tortillas.

5   Pour the remaining enchilada sauce over the tortillas, and bake uncovered for 20 minutes.

insanely easy
To make this in the microwave, prepare the recipe as directed, cover, and microwave on high for 5 minutes.

ingredient tip
Look for Frontera Red Chile Enchilada Sauce to make this dish.

Loaded Sweet Potatoes

Roasted sweet potatoes are the perfect vehicle for . . . well, just about anything! My favorite flavors to serve on them include smoky barbecue sauce, crumbled tempeh, and guacamole.

4 small sweet potatoes, scrubbed and thinly sliced
2 tablespoons canola oil, divided
Sea salt
1 (8-ounce) package tempeh, crumbled
1 cup barbecue sauce
½ cup 5-Minute Guacamole (page 188) or store bought

1   Preheat the oven to 425°F.

2   On a rimmed baking sheet, spread out the sweet potatoes, and toss with 1 tablespoon of oil to coat. Season with salt. Bake for 20 to 25 minutes, or until the bottoms of the sweet potatoes are caramelized and the tops are wilted.

3   Meanwhile, in a large skillet, heat the remaining 1 tablespoon of oil over medium heat. Cook the tempeh until golden brown, about 5 to 7 minutes. Add the barbecue sauce, and continue cooking for 2 more minutes.

4   To serve, divide the sweet potatoes between the serving bowls. Top with the cooked tempeh and sauce, and finish with a scoop of guacamole.

■ VEGAN
■ GLUTEN-FREE

Serves 2

PREP TIME
5 minutes

COOK TIME
25 minutes

PER SERVING
(1½ CUPS)
Calories: 912
Fat: 39g
Carbs: 127g
Fiber: 15g
Protein: 23g

cooking tip
Do not flip the sweet potatoes after seasoning with salt. This helps them brown on the bottoms better.

Roasted Root Vegetable Frittata

Serves 4

PREP TIME
5 minutes

COOK TIME
25 minutes

**PER SERVING
(1 PIECE)**
Calories: 360
Fat: 21g
Carbs: 21g
Fiber: 3g
Protein: 21g

leftovers tip
Reheat leftover slices of frittata, and top with a simple aïoli: Whisk together 1 table-spoon mayonnaise, ¼ teaspoon minced garlic, and 1 teaspoon lemon juice.

Eggs make a delicious dinner, and they're easy to prepare. In this recipe, I pair them with roasted root vegetables and herbs. The protein, fat, and complex carbohydrates make for a filling one-dish meal.

1 pound assorted root vegetables (potatoes, carrots, turnips, or sweet potatoes), cut into 1-inch pieces
1 tablespoon minced herbs (rosemary, thyme, or parsley)
Sea salt
Freshly ground black pepper
2 tablespoons canola oil
8 eggs
½ cup freshly grated Parmesan cheese

1 Preheat the oven to 425°F.

2 In a baking dish, add the root vegetables and herbs. Season with salt and pepper. Drizzle in the canola oil, and toss gently to mix. Roast uncovered for 15 minutes.

3 In a medium bowl, whisk the eggs. Season with salt.

4 Remove the vegetables from the oven, pour the eggs over them, and top with the Parmesan cheese. Bake for another 10 minutes, or until the eggs are set.

Broccoli-Cheddar Quiche

There's something comforting about pie, even when it's not for dessert. In this recipe, broccoli, eggs, and sharp Cheddar cheese fill a rich, buttery puff pastry shell that vegetarians and carnivores alike will swoon for. Serve with a green salad for a complete meal.

1 prepared puff pastry sheet

2 cups frozen broccoli florets, defrosted

1 cup shredded sharp Cheddar cheese

4 eggs, whisked

1 cup milk

¼ teaspoon sea salt

¼ teaspoon freshly ground pepper

1 Preheat the oven to 400°F.

2 Spread the puff pastry sheet into an 8-by-8-inch baking dish.

3 Spread the broccoli florets over the pastry, and sprinkle with the Cheddar cheese.

4 In a medium bowl, whisk together the eggs, milk, salt, and pepper. Pour the egg mixture over the broccoli and cheese.

5 Bake for 20 to 25 minutes, or until the quiche is set. Allow to rest for 5 minutes before slicing and serving

■ VEGETARIAN

Serves 4

PREP TIME
5 minutes

COOK TIME
20 to 25 minutes

**PER SERVING
(1 PIECE)**
Calories: 305
Fat: 20g
Carbs: 13g
Fiber: 1g
Protein: 19g

foodie 101
Puff pastry is a labor-intensive dough made with flour, ice water, and cold butter. As it cooks, the thin layers of butter produce steam and puff the dough, producing a tender, flaky texture.

Thai Peanut Noodles

≡ VEGAN
≡ GLUTEN-FREE

Serves 2

PREP TIME
5 minutes, plus
10 minutes to sit

COOK TIME
5 minutes

**PER SERVING
(1 CUP)**
Calories: 546
Fat: 25g
Carbs: 65g
Fiber: 4g
Protein: 16g

prep tip
To save time, use
precooked lo mein
noodles.

Thai peanut sauce has the perfect balance of salty, sweet, spicy, and savory. To ensure the sauce is vegetarian, read the label, as sometimes it contains fish sauce. Or you can make your own savory peanut sauce with the recipe provided afterward.

4 ounces thin rice noodles
4 cups boiling water
2 tablespoons canola oil
2 eggs, whisked
2 scallions, thinly sliced
1 carrot, shredded
½ cup Thai Peanut Sauce (page 129), or store bought

1 Place the rice noodles in a heatproof dish, and cover with boiling water. Allow to soften for 10 minutes, then drain in a colander.

2 Heat a large skillet over medium heat until hot. Add the canola oil, and heat for 30 seconds. Pour the eggs into the pan. Cook undisturbed for 1 to 2 minutes, until the eggs are set. Carefully flip the egg pancake over, and cook for 30 seconds on the other side. Slide the cooked eggs onto a cutting board.

3 Add the scallions and carrots to the pan, and sauté for 30 seconds. Add the noodles to the pan, and cook for 1 minute. Pour in the peanut sauce, and cook until just heated through.

4 Slice the egg into long, thin strips, and add to the noodles just before serving.

Thai Peanut Sauce: To make your own peanut sauce, in a small jar combine ¼ cup of peanut butter with 2 tablespoons of soy sauce, 1 tablespoon of honey or brown sugar, 2 tablespoons of lime juice, 1 teaspoon of minced ginger, ¼ teaspoon of red pepper flakes, and 1 teaspoon of minced garlic. Cover the jar tightly with a lid, and shake vigorously until combined.

Shakshuka

■ VEGETARIAN
■ GLUTEN-FREE

Serves 2 to 4

PREP TIME
5 minutes

COOK TIME
15 minutes

PER SERVING
(2 EGGS PLUS 1 CUP
VEGETABLES)
Calories: 445
Fat: 33g
Carbs: 23g
Fiber: 6g
Protein: 18g

This one-pan vegetarian meal is perfect for a savory breakfast or a filling dinner. For added protein, consider adding cooked white beans to the pan just before adding the eggs, and top with crumbled feta cheese.

3 tablespoons extra-virgin olive oil
4 garlic cloves, smashed
1 onion, halved and thinly sliced
3 bell peppers, red, yellow, and orange, cored and thinly sliced
1 (15-ounce) can fire-roasted diced tomatoes, drained
Sea salt
Freshly ground black pepper
4 eggs

OPTIONAL ADD-IN
¼ cup roughly chopped fresh parsley, for serving

foodie 101
Shakshuka is traditionally spiced with ground cumin, smoked paprika, and cayenne pepper. If you have these spices in your pantry, add ¼ teaspoon of each to your shakshuka before adding the eggs.

1 In a large skillet, heat the olive oil over medium heat. Cook the garlic and onion for 5 minutes, until they begin to soften.

2 Add the bell peppers and cook for another 5 minutes.

3 Add the tomatoes, and bring to a simmer. Season with salt and pepper.

4 Make four indentations in the vegetable mixture, and crack an egg into each one. Cook uncovered until the whites are set and the egg yolks are still runny, about 5 minutes. Sprinkle with fresh parsley (if using).

Hoisin-Ginger Tofu Stir-Fry

Hoisin sauce is sweet, spicy, and full of flavor. If you follow a gluten-free diet, make sure to check the label. Hoisin usually contains soy sauce and may or may not be made with wheat.

■ **VEGAN**
■ **GLUTEN-FREE**

Serves 2

PREP TIME
10 minutes

COOK TIME
20 minutes

**PER SERVING
(2 CUPS)**
Calories: 386
Fat: 20g
Carbs: 33g
Fiber: 6g
Protein: 23g

2 tablespoons canola oil, divided

1 (16-ounce) package extra-firm tofu, halved horizontally, pressed and drained

4 cups diced assorted vegetables (broccoli, carrots, and sugar snap peas)

1 tablespoon minced ginger

1 tablespoon minced garlic

¼ cup hoisin sauce

1 In a large skillet, heat 1 tablespoon of oil over medium-high heat. Sear the tofu for 5 minutes on each side, or until golden brown. Transfer to a cutting board.

2 Add the remaining 1 tablespoon of oil to the pan, and sauté the vegetables until they're beginning to soften yet still brightly colored, about 10 minutes.

3 Add the ginger and garlic to the pan, and cook for 30 seconds, until just fragrant.

4 Slice the tofu into cubes, and return it to the pan with the vegetables.

5 Add the hoisin sauce, and toss the vegetables and tofu gently to coat in the sauce.

prep tip
To press the tofu, place the two halves between two cutting boards. Place a heavy object on top, and allow the tofu to drain for 10 minutes or more. Pat dry with paper towels.

Eggplant, Bell Pepper, and Pineapple Curry

▪ VEGAN
▪ GLUTEN-FREE

Serves 4

PREP TIME
5 minutes

COOK TIME
25 minutes

PER SERVING
(1 CUP)
Calories: 183
Fat: 8g
Carbs: 24g
Fiber: 7g
Protein: 3g

---

prep tip
Canned pineapple is fine to use in the recipe. Simply drain it, and reserve the syrup for another use.

Curry paste is a wonder ingredient! It's packed with spices and brings so much flavor to this vegetable curry. Use whatever vegetable you have on hand, but I love the pillowy texture of eggplant, the complexity of green bell pepper, and the sweetness of pineapple. For a more savory curry, use 2 cups of diced tomato in place of the pineapple.

1 eggplant, cut into 1-inch cubes
1 green bell pepper, cored and cut into 1-inch pieces
2 cups cubed pineapple
2 (15-ounce) cans light coconut milk
2 tablespoons red curry paste
Sea salt
Freshly ground black pepper

Place all the ingredients in a large pot, and bring to a simmer over medium heat. Cover and cook on low for 25 minutes, or until the vegetables are tender. Season with salt and pepper.

Soba Noodle & Veggie Stir-Fry

There's something to be said for twirling your fork around a savory bowl of pasta. This vegan version is loaded with fresh vegetables and healthy soba noodles, all bathed in a spicy stir-fry sauce.

1 (8-ounce) package soba noodles
2 tablespoons canola oil
1 red bell pepper, thinly sliced
2 cups sugar snap peas, strings removed
2 cups sliced button mushrooms
½ cup General Tso's stir-fry sauce

1 Bring a large pot of salted water to a boil on the stove. Place the soba noodles in it and cooking according to package instructions, about 6 to 8 minutes, then drain.

2 While the soba noodles cook, heat a large skillet over medium-high heat until very hot, about 1 minute. Add the canola oil, and heat for 30 seconds.

3 Sauté the red bell pepper, sugar snap peas, and mushrooms for 3 to 5 minutes, until slightly softened.

4 Add the cooked and drained noodles to the pan, and sauté for 1 to 2 minutes. Add the stir-fry sauce, and cook for 30 seconds. Give everything a good toss, and divide between the serving bowls.

ingredient tip: A great brand of stir-fry sauce to look for is House of Tsang General Tso Stir-Fry Sauce, with no monosodium glutamate or high-fructose corn syrup.

■ **VEGETARIAN**

Serves 2

PREP TIME
5 minutes

COOK TIME
20 minutes

**PER SERVING
(2 CUPS)**
Calories: 392
Fat: 17g
Carbs: 50g
Fiber: 5g
Protein 12g

prep tip
To remove the strings from the snap peas, use a paring knife to slice the stem end, and peel the string away from one side.

LEMON CHICKEN
(PAGE 146)

Chapter 7

SEAFOOD AND POULTRY MAINS

Shrimp Scampi

Shrimp is inexpensive and easy to find in the frozen section of the grocery store. It is high in protein and low in fat, making it a healthy option. It is also incredibly versatile and can be enjoyed on salads, in pasta dishes, and simply dipped in cocktail sauce.

Serves 4

PREP TIME
10 minutes

COOK TIME
10 minutes

**PER SERVING
(1½ CUPS)**
Calories: 376
Fat: 13g
Carbs: 45g
Fiber: 2g
Protein: 23g

8 ounces linguine noodles
Sea salt
3 tablespoons extra-virgin olive oil
4 garlic cloves, minced
2 shallots, minced
1 pound shrimp, peeled
Freshly ground black pepper
3 tablespoons freshly squeezed lemon juice

OPTIONAL ADD-INS
¼ cup minced fresh parsley
½ cup finely grated Parmesan cheese

1   Heat a large pot of salted water over high heat. Cook the linguine according to the package instructions, about 7 to 9 minutes. Drain in a colander.

2   In a large skillet, heat the olive oil over medium heat.

3   Add the garlic and shallot to the pan, and cook for 2 minutes. Add the shrimp to the pan, and cook for 3 to 4 minutes, or until just cooked through and opaque. Season with salt and pepper.

4   Transfer the cooked pasta to the skillet, and sauté for 1 minute. Shower with the lemon juice. Top with the fresh parsley and Parmesan cheese (if using).

VARIATIONS

Shrimp Cocktail: Bring a large pot of salted water to a boil. Add 1 pound of shrimp with the tails on. Simmer for 2 minutes, or until the shrimp turn opaque and form a C shape. Drain in a colander, and rinse with cool water. Use store-bought cocktail sauce, or make a quick cocktail sauce with ½ cup ketchup, 1 tablespoon horseradish, 1 teaspoon Worcestershire sauce, and 1 teaspoon lemon juice. Season with salt and lots of black pepper.

Shrimp Fajitas: Heat 2 tablespoons of canola oil in a large skillet over medium-high heat. Sauté 1 yellow onion, sliced, and 2 bell peppers (any color), cored and sliced, for 2 minutes. Add 1 tablespoon of chili powder or taco seasoning and 1 pound of peeled shrimp. Cook for another 2 minutes, or until the shrimp are opaque. Season with salt and pepper. Serve with flour tortillas and 5-Minute Guacamole (page 188).

ingredient tip
Shrimp is sold according to how many shrimp are in each pound. Hence, a label that reads "26/30" contains roughly 26 to 30 shrimp per pound. As the numbers go down, the size of the shrimp—not to mention the price—increases.

Honey-Soy Salmon

■ GLUTEN-FREE
OPTION
■ MICROWAVE
FRIENDLY

Serves 4

PREP TIME
5 minutes

COOK TIME
12 minutes

**PER SERVING
(4-OUNCE FILLET)**
Calories: 338
Fat: 19g
Carbs: 19g
Fiber: 0g
Protein: 24g

This recipe has the perfect balance of sweet, salty, spicy, and sour flavors. To deepen these flavors, allow the fish to sit in the marinade in the refrigerator for 30 minutes before baking. Serve it with steamed vegetables and rice for a complete meal.

¼ cup honey
¼ cup soy sauce
2 tablespoons canola oil
1 tablespoon freshly squeezed lime juice
1 tablespoon minced ginger
Sea salt
Freshly ground black pepper
1 large salmon fillet, about 1 pound

1 Preheat the oven to 400°F.

2 In an 8-by-8-inch square baking dish, whisk together the honey, soy sauce, canola oil, lime juice, and ginger. Season with salt and pepper.

3 Place the salmon into the honey-soy mixture, and turn to coat all sides.

4 Bake uncovered for 12 minutes, or until the fish flakes easily with a fork.

insanely easy
Combine all the ingredients in a microwave-safe dish, cover, and cook on high for 6 minutes, or until the fish flakes easily with a fork.

substitution tip
To make this gluten-free, use a gluten-free soy sauce.

Tomato-Basil Braised Cod

This aromatic, mildly spiced tomato-basil sauce is the perfect complement to cod. Cod is a good choice because it is available year-round in the frozen-foods section of the grocery store for a fraction of the cost of other fish. Braising is a technique for cooking food partially submerged in a sauce, whereas poaching involves submerging food in liquid and cooking at the barest simmer.

3 tablespoons extra-virgin olive oil

4 garlic cloves, minced

1 pint cherry tomatoes, halved

1 cup roughly chopped fresh basil leaves

Zest and juice of 1 lemon

2 cod fillets, about 8 ounces each

Sea salt

Freshly ground black pepper

1 In a large skillet, heat the olive oil over medium heat. Add the garlic, and cook for 1 minute, until fragrant.

2 Add the tomatoes, and cook for 10 minutes, until soft and juicy.

3 Stir in the basil, lemon zest, and lemon juice, and lower the heat to bring to a simmer.

4 Season the cod fillets with salt and pepper, and place them in the tomato-basil mixture. Cook for 5 minutes, then flip and cook for another 5 minutes, or until cooked through.

■ GLUTEN-FREE

■ MICROWAVE FRIENDLY

Serves 2

PREP TIME
10 minutes

COOK TIME
20 minutes

PER SERVING
(8-OUNCE FILLET)
Calories: 415
Fat: 23g
Carbs: 10g
Fiber: 2g
Protein: 44g

prep tip
To cook this in the microwave, combine all the ingredients in a microwave-safe dish, cover, and cook on high for 6 minutes, or until the fish flakes easily with a fork.

Spicy Shrimp and Soba Noodles

Serves 4

PREP TIME
5 minutes

COOK TIME
15 minutes

PER SERVING
(1½ CUPS)
Calories: 344
Fat: 9g
Carbs: 46g
Fiber: 0g
Protein: 25g

ingredient tip
Soba is a Japanese pasta made with buckwheat, which is naturally gluten-free. However, wheat flour is sometimes added during processing. Look for the words "100% buckwheat" on the package to know the noodles are gluten-free.

This riff on street noodles is easy to whip up between classes. It's a perfect recipe for carb loading before an athletic event, and the soba noodles provide all eight essential amino acids to help rebuild and repair muscle. For a little more color, texture, and nutrition, add a handful of sliced carrots, mushrooms, and bell peppers to the mix.

1 (8-ounce package) soba noodles
2 tablespoons canola oil
1 pound jumbo shrimp, peeled
1 tablespoon minced garlic
¼ teaspoon red pepper flakes
¼ cup soy sauce

1 Bring a large pot of salted water to a boil, and cook the soba noodles according to the package instructions, about 7 to 9 minutes. Drain thoroughly.

2 In a large skillet, heat the canola oil, and fry the shrimp for 2 minutes, until nearly cooked through.

3 Add the garlic and red pepper flakes. Cook for 30 seconds, then add the noodles and soy sauce.

4 Sauté for 1 minute, or until the shrimp are fully cooked and the noodles are coated in sauce.

Crab and Artichoke Linguine

Crab, mint, and artichoke is a fresh flavor medley that can be adapted to a wide variety of applications, from appetizers to casseroles. My favorite combination is to serve them with pasta, as it comes together quickly and easily. Serve with lemon wedges on the side.

8 ounces linguine noodles
¼ cup extra-virgin olive oil
1 pound lump crabmeat, picked over for shells
1 (12-ounce) jar marinated artichoke hearts
¼ cup roughly chopped fresh mint
¼ cup finely grated Parmesan cheese
Sea salt
Freshly ground black pepper

1 Bring a large pot of salted water to a boil. Cook the linguine according to the package instructions until al dente, about 7 to 9 minutes. Drain in a colander.

2 In the same pot, add the olive oil, crabmeat, and artichoke hearts, and sauté until just heated through.

3 Return the pasta to the pot, and add the mint and Parmesan cheese. Season with salt and pepper and toss.

■ GOOD FOR SHARING

Serves 4

PREP TIME
5 minutes

COOK TIME
15 minutes

PER SERVING
(1½ CUPS)
Calories: 535
Fat: 22g
Carbs: 52g
Fiber: 6g
Protein: 33g

foodie 101
Artichoke hearts come from the tender inner portion of the artichoke. Using whole, fresh artichokes is labor intensive and expensive, so it is one of the few vegetables I prefer buying canned.

Tuna Cakes with Potato Skins

▪ GLUTEN-FREE

Serves 4

PREP TIME
10 minutes

COOK TIME
30 minutes

PER SERVING
(2 TUNA CAKES AND
1 POTATO SKIN)
Calories: 290
Fat: 15g
Carbs: 17g
Fiber: 1g
Protein: 24g

I developed this recipe while visiting my younger brother in Italy. When I foraged through his bachelor pad pantry, I found Honey Nut Cheerios, canned tuna, and spinach—not exactly dinner material. But I had used canned seafood to make crab and salmon cakes, so why not tuna? Turns out, it was really good! This version uses potatoes as a binder, so it's naturally gluten-free, and you can make a delicious side dish out of the potato skins.

2 small russet potatoes, scrubbed
3 tablespoons extra-virgin olive oil, divided
Sea salt
Freshly ground black pepper
2 (6-ounce) cans water-packed tuna
1 egg
1 scallion, thinly sliced
1 lemon, cut into wedges, for serving

1. Preheat the oven to 400°F.

2. Pierce the potatoes several times with a fork. Place them in the microwave, and cook on high for 2 to 3 minutes. Turn them over, and microwave for another 2 minutes, or until cooked through.

3. Allow the potatoes to cool slightly. Slice in quarters lengthwise. Scoop the potato flesh from the quarters, and transfer to a small mixing bowl.

4   Place the potato skins on a rimmed baking sheet. Brush with 1 tablespoon of olive oil, and season generously with salt and pepper. Bake for 20 minutes, or until golden and crisp.

5   To the mixing bowl with the potato, add the tuna, egg, and scallion. Mash gently to mix. Season with salt and pepper.

6   In a large skillet, heat the remaining 2 tablespoons of oil over medium heat.

7   Form the tuna mixture into 8 small balls, and flatten gently with your hands. Fry the cakes on each side for 3 to 4 minutes, flipping gently, or until golden brown on the bottom. Serve with the potato skins.

leftovers tip
You can freeze leftover tuna cakes in a zip-top plastic bag. Bake them from frozen for 20 minutes to serve.

Ham-Stuffed Chicken Breast

Serves 2

PREP TIME
5 minutes

COOK TIME
25 minutes

**PER SERVING
(1 CHICKEN BREAST)**
Calories: 405
Fat: 13g
Carbs: 29g
Fiber: 2g
Protein: 43g

This is a simplified version of the classic chicken cordon bleu. It makes a quick and easy dinner with only a few minutes of prep time. You can also prepare it in a skillet on the stove. Heat the oil in a large skillet, and sear on each side for 10 minutes, until cooked through.

2 boneless, skinless chicken breasts
2 slices deli ham
2 slices Swiss cheese
½ cup panko bread crumbs
Sea salt
Freshly ground black pepper
1 egg, whisked

1 Preheat the oven to 400°F.

2 Slice the chicken breasts nearly in half horizontally so that one side remains attached. Open the chicken breasts as if you're opening a book, and layer each with 1 slice of ham and 1 slice of Swiss cheese. Close each chicken breast, and press to seal the edges, holding it in place with a toothpick.

3 Combine the bread crumbs, salt, and pepper in a shallow dish.

4 Dip the stuffed chicken in the egg, shaking off any excess, and roll in the bread-crumb mixture to coat. Place the chicken breast in a baking dish, and repeat with the second chicken breast.

5 Bake for 25 minutes, until the chicken is cooked through and the cheese is melted.

Cheesy Stuffed Chicken in Salsa Verde: Follow the recipe as directed, but stuff the chicken breasts with a mixture of ¼ cup of minced cilantro, 4 ounces of cream cheese, and ½ cup of fire-roasted tomatoes. Place the stuffed chicken breasts in the baking dish, and top with 2 cups of salsa verde.

Pan-Seared Chicken with Zucchini: Place the chicken breasts between two sheets of parchment paper, and using a heavy pan, pound the breasts until they are a uniform thickness, about ½ to ¾ inch. Season generously with salt and pepper. Heat 2 tablespoons of canola oil over medium heat until hot. Sear the chicken for about 5 to 7 minutes on each side, until cooked through and well browned. Transfer the chicken to a serving platter. Add 2 cups of diced zucchini to the pan, and sauté for 3 to 4 minutes, until browned and just beginning to soften. Season generously with salt and pepper.

Chicken with Mushrooms and Onions: Place the chicken breasts between two sheets of parchment paper, and using a heavy pan, pound the breasts until they are a uniform thickness, about ½ inch. Season generously with salt and pepper. Heat 2 tablespoons of canola oil over medium heat until hot. Sear the chicken for about 5 minutes on one side. Flip the chicken and add 1 cup of sliced mushrooms and ½ cup of thinly sliced onions to the pan. Cover the pan, and cook for 5 to 7 minutes. Transfer the chicken to a serving platter, and top with the mushrooms and onions.

prep tip
Purchase prepared bread crumbs, or to make your own, toast 2 slices of bread in a toaster, and place them in a food processor and pulse until coarsely ground.

Lemon Chicken

Serves 2

PREP TIME
5 minutes

COOK TIME
25 minutes

**PER SERVING:
(2 DRUMSTICKS)**
Calories: 400
Fat: 31g
Carbs: 4g
Fiber: 0g
Protein: 28g

prep tip
To ensure a nice brown crust, make sure to dry the meat thoroughly before placing it in a hot skillet. Moisture hinders the process because it produces steam.

Each tender, juicy bite of these drumsticks is offset by crispy and delicious skin, and a savory pan sauce.

2 tablespoons canola oil
4 bone-in, skin-on chicken drumsticks
Sea salt
Freshly ground black pepper
1 head garlic, halved
Zest and juice of 1 lemon, plus 1 lemon, halved
1 fresh rosemary sprig
2 tablespoons butter

1 Preheat the oven to 400°F.

2 In a large skillet, heat the oil over medium-high heat. Pat the chicken dry with paper towels, and season with salt and pepper. Place the chicken in the pan, skin-side down. Add the garlic and lemon halves to the pan, and the rosemary. Sear the chicken for 5 to 7 minutes, until a nice brown crust forms. Flip the chicken, and cook on the other side for 5 minutes.

3 Cover the skillet and lower the heat to medium-low. Cook for 10 minutes, or until the chicken is cooked through to an internal temperature of 165°F. Remove the chicken to a cutting board.

4 Add the lemon zest, lemon juice, and butter to the pan, and whisk to make a quick sauce from the pan juices. Remove the rosemary sprig.

5 Serve the chicken drumsticks with the pan sauce.

Chicken Provençal

Zucchini, tomatoes, onions, and herbs are the primary ingredients in ratatouille, a rustic French dish that usually includes eggplant as well. Here, the vegetables form a bright, flavorful backdrop for pan-seared chicken thighs. Make sure to serve this with a generous slice of whole-grain bread and with olive oil and balsamic vinegar for dipping.

2 tablespoons extra-virgin olive oil
1 pound boneless, skinless chicken thighs
Sea salt
Freshly ground black pepper
1 small yellow onion, minced
1 zucchini, diced
1 pint cherry tomatoes
½ teaspoon dried rosemary

1 In a large skillet, heat the olive oil over medium-high heat. Season the chicken thighs with salt and pepper. Sear the chicken for 5 minutes on one side.

2 Flip the chicken to the other side, and add the onion, zucchini, tomatoes, and rosemary. Bring to a simmer, and cook for 15 minutes, until the vegetables are tender and the chicken is cooked through.

■ GLUTEN-FREE

Serves 2

PREP TIME
5 minutes

COOK TIME
20 minutes

PER SERVING
(ABOUT 2 THIGHS)
Calories: 441
Fat: 24g
Carbs: 11g
Fiber: 3g
Protein: 47g

substitution tip
Fresh and dried herbs can be used interchangeably in most recipes; however, the amount used will differ. In most recipes, you will want to use about three times the amount of a fresh herbs as you would dried.

Coriander-Crusted Chicken Breasts

■ GLUTEN-FREE

Serves 4

PREP TIME
10 minutes

COOK TIME
20 minutes

PER SERVING
(1 BREAST)
Calories: 183
Fat: 9g
Carbs: 5g
Fiber: 1g
Protein: 24g

Freshly ground black pepper and coriander form a delicious, crispy crust on the chicken. The coating can also be used for salmon. If you don't happen to have, or want to buy, whole coriander and peppercorns, see the tip for an easy substitution. Serve with a simple side salad and steamed rice for a complete meal.

1 tablespoon whole coriander seeds

1 tablespoon whole peppercorns

1 teaspoon sea salt

2 tablespoons canola oil

4 boneless, skinless chicken breasts

1 red onion, halved and thinly sliced

1 (15-ounce) can whole plum tomatoes, drained

1. Place the coriander and peppercorns into a large zip-top plastic bag. Using a heavy pot, break apart the spices until they are coarsely ground. Mix in the sea salt.

2. Place the chicken breasts between two sheets of parchment paper, and using a heavy pan, pound the breasts until they are a uniform thickness, about ½ to ¾ inch. Place the chicken in the zip-top bag, and coat the chicken in the spice mixture.

3 In a large skillet, heat the oil over medium-high heat.

4 Place the chicken in the pan, and cook for 5 minutes, until a nice golden crust forms. Flip the chicken breasts, and cook on the other side for 2 to 3 minutes.

5 Add the sliced onion to the pan, and cook for another 5 minutes.

6 Using a spoon, break apart the tomatoes in the can, and add to the pan; bring to a simmer. Cook for 5 minutes, or until the chicken is cooked through.

substitution tip
While there's no doubting the deliciousness of a coriander and peppercorn crust, you can make another great crusted chicken recipe with panko bread crumbs and Parmesan in their place. Swap out the coriander seeds and peppercorns and instead use ¾ cup panko bread crumbs and ¼ cup grated Parmesan cheese. Eliminate the sea salt, as the Parm will make it unncessary. To keep the recipe gluten-free, look for gluten-free panko bread crumbs.

Creamy Chicken and Mushroom Fettuccine

Serves 4

PREP TIME
10 minutes

COOK TIME
13 minutes

PER SERVING
(1½ CUPS)
Calories: 368
Fat: 13g
Carbs: 44g
Fiber: 2g
Protein: 22g

If you're looking for a way to liven up a basic chicken dinner, take a cue from French cooking. Chicken, mushrooms, and cream appear throughout the country's culinary tradition and bring an extra layer of luxury to dinner. In this recipe, I lighten things up with half-and-half and let it infuse with the shallot and mushrooms for extra flavor.

1 (8-ounce package) fettuccine noodles
2 tablespoons canola oil
4 boneless, skinless chicken thighs, sliced in 2-inch pieces
Sea salt
Freshly ground black pepper
1 cup thinly sliced cremini mushrooms
1 shallot, minced
¼ cup half-and-half

1 Bring a large pot of salted water to a boil. Cook the fettuccine according to the package instructions, 7 to 9 minutes. Drain in a colander.

2 In a large skillet, heat the canola oil over medium-high heat. Pat the chicken thigh slices dry with a paper towel. Season generously with salt and pepper.

3   Sear the chicken for 3 to 4 minutes, then flip the pieces.

4   Add the mushrooms and shallots to the pan. Cook for another 3 to 4 minutes, turning the mushrooms to brown on both sides.

5   Pour the half-and-half into the pan, reduce the heat to low, and simmer for 2 to 3 minutes, basting the chicken with the sauce. Season with salt and pepper.

6   Add the cooked pasta to the pan, and toss gently to coat in the sauce.

prep tip
This recipe cooks quickly, so have all the ingredients measured and ready to cook before you begin.

Shredded-Chicken Street Tacos

▪ GLUTEN-FREE

Serves 4

PREP TIME
5 minutes

COOK TIME
15 minutes

PER SERVING
(2 TACOS)
Calories: 464
Fat: 13g
Carbs: 73g
Fiber: 14g
Protein: 27g

I learned to make these shredded-chicken tacos at a cooking school in England, of all places. But the flavors are straight out of Latin America. Serve with thinly sliced red onion, plum tomatoes, and a dollop of 5-Minute Guacamole (page 188).

4 garlic cloves, finely minced
1 tablespoon chili powder
½ teaspoon sea salt
2 tablespoons canola oil
4 bone-in, skin-on chicken thighs
1 (15-ounce) can crushed tomatoes
1 tablespoon red wine vinegar
8 corn tortillas

1   In a small bowl, mash the garlic, chili powder, and salt into a thick paste. Spread this onto the skin-side of the chicken.

2   In a large skillet, heat the canola oil over medium heat until hot. Place the chicken skin-side down in the oil, and fry for 3 to 5 minutes, or until a nice crust forms. Make sure not to burn the garlic.

3 Flip the chicken, and add the crushed tomatoes and red wine vinegar. Cover the pot, and simmer for 10 minutes, or until the chicken is cooked through.

4 Transfer the chicken to a cutting board, and allow it to rest for 10 minutes, or until cool enough to handle. Use a fork to remove the meat from the bones and shred the meat. Return the meat to the cooking pot, and mix to combine.

5 Place a spoonful of the shredded chicken into each of the corn tortillas and serve.

prep tip

The garlic should be minced as finely as possible for this recipe. A fine grater or a mortar and pestle work well, but if you don't have one of these tools, use the side of your chef's knife to smash the garlic into a paste.

Teriyaki Chicken Bowl

■ GOOD FOR
SHARING

Serves 2

PREP TIME
5 minutes

COOK TIME
20 minutes

PER SERVING
(¾ CUP TERIYAKI
CHICKEN AND
1 CUP RICE)
Calories: 744
Fat: 11g
Carbs: 100g
Fiber: 3g
Protein: 62g

In college I wrote for an Asian newspaper in Portland. Nearly every day the owner of the paper cooked lunch in the on-site kitchen for the staff. Teriyaki sauce, meat, and steamed rice were on the menu most days. The meal came together quickly and filled the office with delicious smells, just as this dish will when you fix it.

1 cup white rice

1½ cups water

Sea salt

1 tablespoon canola oil

1 pound chicken tenders

Freshly ground black pepper

1 red bell pepper, cored and thinly sliced

1 cup teriyaki sauce

OPTIONAL ADD-IN

3 baby bok choy, thinly sliced

1 In a pot, add the white rice, the water, and a pinch of sea salt. Bring to a simmer, cover, and cook on low for 15 minutes, or until all the liquid is absorbed.

2 In a large skillet, heat the oil over medium-high heat. Pat the chicken tenders dry with paper towels, and season with salt and pepper. Cook, flipping once, for 7 to 10 minutes, until cooked through and well browned. Transfer the meat to a separate dish.

3 Place the red pepper and bok choy (if using) in the pan, and sauté for 2 to 3 minutes, until the bok choy is bright green and wilted.

4 Return the chicken to the pan along with the teriyaki sauce, and simmer everything for 1 to 2 minutes, until the sauce is heated through. Serve over the steamed rice.

foodie 101
As its name suggests, baby bok choy is a smaller version of the vegetable bok choy. It is crunchy with a bright, slightly bitter flavor.

ingredient tip
Look for House of Tsang Korean Teriyaki Sauce when making this dish.

Thai Ginger Chicken

GLUTEN-FREE

Serves 2

PREP TIME
5 minutes

COOK TIME
15 minutes

**PER SERVING
(1 CHICKEN BREAST)**
Calories: 295
Fat: 23g
Carbs: 4g
Fiber: 1g
Protein: 23g

substitution tip
You can replace the ginger with 1 table-spoon of minced lemongrass for an exotic twist. To prepare the lemon-grass, remove the tough outer layers. Slice off the root end and most of the stalk, leaving about 2 inches of the ten-der inner portion. Cut the lemongrass perpendicular to the stalk in thin rounds.

One of my favorite restaurants in college was called Thai Ginger, and my favorite recipe on its menu was a flavorful chicken salad. Serve this spicy chicken atop a bed of mixed greens, with an extra drizzle of lime juice and a side of steamed rice.

3 tablespoons canola oil
2 boneless, skinless chicken breasts
Sea salt
Freshly ground black pepper
Pinch red pepper flakes
1 tablespoon minced ginger
2 shallots, minced
2 tablespoons lime juice, plus more for serving

1 In a large skillet, heat the canola oil over medium-high heat. Pat the chicken breasts dry with a paper towel. Season generously with salt and pepper.

2 Sear the chicken on one side for 5 minutes. Flip the chicken to the other side, and cook for 5 minutes, or until cooked through. Transfer the cooked chicken to a cutting board to rest.

3 Reduce the heat to medium-low. Add the red pepper flakes, ginger, and shallots to the pan, and cook for 2 minutes. Add the lime juice, and cook for another 30 seconds. Spoon this mixture over the cooked chicken breasts to serve.

Chicken, Sausage, and White Bean Cassoulet

To the French food purists out there, I'm sorry. This isn't a traditional method for preparing cassoulet. However, it does have all the basic elements—pork, poultry, and beans simmered in a richly flavored pan sauce. Whatever you call it, sop up the delicious juices with a big hunk of crusty bread.

2 tablespoons canola oil
4 boneless, skinless chicken thighs
Sea salt
Freshly ground black pepper
2 garlic pork sausages, cut into 2-inch pieces
1 cup chicken broth
2 fresh thyme sprigs
1 (15-ounce) can cannellini beans, drained and rinsed

1 Heat the canola oil in a large skillet over medium-high heat. Pat the chicken dry with paper towels, and season generously with salt and pepper. Place the chicken in the pan, and sear for 5 minutes.

2 Flip the chicken, and add the pork sausages to the pan. Cook for 5 more minutes.

3 Add the chicken broth, thyme, and cannellini beans to the pan, and simmer uncovered for another 10 minutes, until the chicken and sausages are cooked through. Allow to rest for 5 minutes, remove the thyme sprigs, and serve.

■ GLUTEN-FREE

Serves 4

PREP TIME
5 minutes

COOK TIME
20 minutes

PER SERVING
(1 CUP)
Calories: 285
Fat: 14g
Carbs: 16g
Fiber: 4g
Protein: 22g

foodie 101
Traditional French cassoulet is made with pork sausages, duck, white beans, and goose fat.

HOMEMADE MEATBALLS
(PAGE 164)

Chapter 8

PORK AND BEEF MAINS

Fried Rice

- GLUTEN-FREE OPTION
- GOOD FOR SHARING

Serves 2

PREP TIME
5 minutes

COOK TIME
15 minutes

**PER SERVING
(1½ CUPS)**
Calories: 451
Fat: 6g
Carbs: 84g
Fiber: 4g
Protein: 15g

substitution tip
To make this dish
gluten-free, use
a gluten-free
soy sauce.

This is one of my favorite ways to enjoy leftover rice. It's a resourceful way to use up those soy sauce packets and steamed rice that come with Chinese takeout. You can also use brown rice if you want to add more fiber.

2 slices bacon, cut into small pieces
1 tablespoon minced garlic
2 cups cooked rice, cooled
1 cup frozen peas and carrots, defrosted
2 tablespoons soy sauce or gluten-free tamari

1   In a large skillet, cook the bacon pieces over medium-low heat until the bacon renders most of its fat and is cooked through, about 10 minutes. Transfer the cooked bacon to a separate dish.

2   Cook the ginger in the bacon fat for 30 seconds until fragrant. Add the rice and peas and carrots, stirring continuously, and cook for 2 minutes, allowing the rice to soak up the bacon fat.

3   Return the cooked bacon to the pan, and add the soy sauce. Stir and cook for 1 minute before serving.

Italian Sausage, Pepper, and Onion Skillet

This one-pan meal is ready in a flash and bursting with flavor from spicy Italian sausage, sweet bell peppers, and savory onions. You can serve it over pasta or on a bed of mixed greens for a low-carb option.

1 tablespoon canola oil
4 hot Italian sausage links, cut into 1-inch pieces
2 bell peppers, green and red, cored and thinly sliced
1 yellow onion, halved and thinly sliced
2 garlic cloves, roughly chopped
Sea salt
Freshly ground black pepper
1 tablespoon red wine vinegar

1   In a large skillet, heat the canola oil over medium-high heat. Add the sausage pieces, and cook for 5 minutes, until they begin to brown.

2   Add the peppers and onion, and cook for another 5 to 7 minutes, or until the vegetables are beginning to soften and the sausage is cooked through.

3   Add the garlic to the pan, and cook for another 30 seconds. Season with salt and pepper. Add a splash of red wine vinegar, and give everything a good toss before serving.

■ GLUTEN-FREE

Serves 4

PREP TIME
10 minutes

COOK TIME
15 minutes

PER SERVING
(1 CUP)
Calories: 315
Fat: 25g
Carbs: 8g
Fiber: 2g
Protein: 17g

insanely easy
You can also make this in the oven. Combine all the ingredients except the vinegar, season with salt and pepper, and roast at 400°F for 25 minutes. Drizzle with the vinegar just before serving.

Pork Chops with Onions and Apples

■ GLUTEN-FREE

Serves 2

PREP TIME
5 minutes

COOK TIME
25 minutes

**PER SERVING
(1 PORK CHOP)**
Calories: 464
Fat: 21g
Carbs: 30g
Fiber: 3g
Protein: 40g

Pork and fruit pair beautifully together, and the meat often appears with apples, pears, figs, raisins, and dates. In this recipe, bone-in pork chops are cooked with stewed onions, apples, apple juice, and thyme for a sweet and savory entrée that locks in the flavor. It's perfect for chilly fall and winter evenings.

2 tablespoons canola oil
2 bone-in pork chops, about 6 to 8 ounces each
Sea salt
Freshly ground black pepper
1 red onion, halved and thinly sliced
1 apple, peeled, cored, and thinly sliced
1 teaspoon fresh thyme leaves
1 cup apple juice

1 In a large skillet, heat the canola oil over medium-high heat.

2 Pat the pork chops dry with paper towels, and season with salt and pepper. Place them in the pan, and sear for 5 minutes.

3 Flip the pork chops, and add the onion to the pan. Cook for 5 minutes.

4 Add the apple, thyme, and apple juice to the pan, and bring to a simmer. Cook for 15 minutes, or until the pork chops are cooked through and the onion and apple are soft.

Brown Sugar–Glazed Ham

This is one of the first entrées I cooked for friends in college. I served it with Green Bean and Apple Salad with Almonds (page 84) and Orange Chocolate Cake (page 182). You can swap the brown sugar for honey or maple syrup if that is what you have on hand.

1- to 1½-pound ham

1 tablespoon whole cloves

¼ cup orange juice

2 tablespoons brown sugar

1 teaspoon hot sauce, such as Cholula Hot Sauce

1 Preheat the oven to 400°F.

2 Score the ham in a diamond pattern, making several incisions at 1-inch intervals with a paring knife. Stick the cloves into the cuts in the meat. Roast the ham for 15 minutes.

3 Whisk together the orange juice, brown sugar, and hot sauce. Brush this over the ham, and return to the oven for 10 minutes, until heated through and bubbling.

GLUTEN-FREE

GOOD FOR SHARING

Serves 4

PREP TIME
5 minutes

COOK TIME
25 minutes

PER SERVING
(¾ CUP)
Calories: 226
Fat: 10g
Carbs: 6g
Fiber: 0g
Protein: 26g

leftovers tip
This ham makes delicious sliced meat for sandwiches. It can also be diced and added to omelets.

Homemade Meatballs

■ GOOD FOR
SHARING

Serves 4

PREP TIME
5 minutes

COOK TIME
15 minutes

PER SERVING
(1 MEATBALL)
Calories: 421
Fat: 32g
Carbs: 10g
Fiber: 1g
Protein: 23g

These classic meatballs are especially tender and juicy. The same technique can be used to make meatloaf. See the variations for a recipe. Serve these meatballs on their own, or add to the Spaghetti Marinara (page 112) for a classic pasta dinner.

1 pound ground beef
1 egg, whisked
1 tablespoon Italian seasoning
½ cup bread crumbs
½ teaspoon sea salt
¼ teaspoon freshly ground black pepper
2 tablespoons canola oil

1 In a large mixing bowl, combine the beef, egg, Italian seasoning, bread crumbs, salt, and pepper. Use your hands to mix.

2 Form the meat mixture into four 2-inch balls, and set aside while the pan heats in the next step.

3 In a large skillet, heat the oil over medium-high heat. Place the meatballs in the skillet, and cook for 15 minutes, turning carefully until browned on all sides and cooked through.

Meatloaf: Don't feel like cooking the meatballs up individually? Pack the meat mixture into a loaf pan, and bake for 45 minutes for a delicious meatloaf. Serve with a side of ketchup.

Tacos: Cook ¼ cup of minced onion with 1 tablespoon of canola oil for 5 minutes, until soft. Add 1 pound of ground beef and 2 tablespoons of taco seasoning. Cook for 5 to 7 minutes, until the beef is cooked through. Stir in ½ cup of ketchup, and cook until thick and bubbling, another 2 minutes.

Skillet Shepherd's Pie: Preheat the oven to 400°F, and oil an 8-by-8-inch baking dish. Heat a large skillet over medium-high heat, and cook 1 pound of ground beef and 1 cup of minced onion for 5 minutes, until cooked through. Season with salt and pepper. Add 2 cups of frozen peas and carrots to the pan, and transfer the mixture to the prepared baking dish. Spread 4 cups prepared mashed potatoes over the meat. Top with 1 cup shredded Cheddar cheese. Bake uncovered for 20 minutes, until the cheese is melted and the casserole is heated through.

Chimichurri Beef

Grassy fresh parsley, fresh cilantro, and red wine vinegar permeate the meat with South American flavors in this easy baked-beef dish. Serve with steamed rice.

■ GLUTEN-FREE
■ GOOD FOR
  SHARING

Serves 4

PREP TIME
10 minutes

COOK TIME
15 minutes

PER SERVING
Calories: 304
Fat: 22g
Carbs: 2g
Fiber: 1g
Protein: 26g

substitution tip
Rather than baking the meat, you can thread it on skewers, and cook it on the grill.

1 cup fresh parsley
1 cup fresh cilantro
2 garlic cloves
2 tablespoons red wine vinegar
¼ cup canola oil
Sea salt
Freshly ground black pepper
1 pound beef tenderloin, cut into 1-inch cubes

1 Preheat the oven to 400°F.

2 In a blender jar, combine the parsley, cilantro, garlic, red wine vinegar, and oil. Purée until mostly smooth, scraping down the sides as needed. Season with salt and pepper.

3 In a medium nonreactive bowl, add the beef cubes, and pour half of the chimichurri mixture over the meat. Use your hands to mix gently. Set the meat aside for 10 minutes to marinate in the sauce.

4 Place the meat on a rimmed baking sheet, and bake for 15 to 20 minutes, or until cooked to your desired level of doneness, about 15 minutes for medium-rare. Serve with the remaining chimichurri sauce on the side.

Steak Fajitas

This one-pan dinner is loaded with flavor and provides satiating protein and complex carbs for a filling meal. Once you have the gist of the basic recipe, you can swap the beef for chicken, shrimp, pork, or vegetarian options such as seitan, tofu, or tempeh. To cool things down, serve with guacamole and sour cream.

- GLUTEN-FREE
- GOOD FOR SHARING

Serves 4

PREP TIME
5 minutes

COOK TIME
15 minutes

PER SERVING (3 FAJITAS)
Calories: 411
Fat: 19g
Carbs: 37g
Fiber: 2g
Protein: 26g

2 tablespoons canola oil, divided
1 pound skirt steak
Sea salt
Freshly ground black pepper
1 yellow onion, thinly sliced
3 bell peppers, green, red, and yellow
1 tablespoon chili powder
12 corn tortillas, warmed

1 In a large skillet, heat 1 tablespoon of oil over medium-high heat. Pat the steak dry with paper towels, and season with salt and pepper. Sear each side for 3 to 5 minutes for medium-rare. Transfer to a cutting board to rest for 5 minutes.

2 Add the onion and peppers to the pan, and sauté for 5 minutes until barely tender.

3 Thinly slice the beef on a bias, and return it along with any accumulated juices to the pan along with the chili powder. Cook for about 1 minute, until the spices are distributed. Season with salt and pepper.

4 Serve with warmed corn tortillas.

leftovers tip
Freeze individual portions of leftover cooked beef and vegetables in zip-top plastic bags for quick meals later on.

Potato, Beef, and Mushroom Casserole

≡ GOOD FOR SHARING

Serves 4

PREP TIME
5 minutes

COOK TIME
25 minutes

PER SERVING (1 PIECE)
Calories: 485
Fat: 30g
Carbs: 29g
Fiber: 4g
Protein: 23g

prep tip
While you probably won't have leftovers if you're sharing this meal with friends, you can also prepare it in individual baking dishes and heat them when you're ready to eat. Increase the cooking time by 5 to 10 minutes if you're cooking from chilled.

This is a healthy version of the classic tater tot casserole. It has all the flavors of the original, with a fraction of the fat and sodium. Choose a low-sodium cream of mushroom soup with an ingredient list you can easily pronounce. To save time, purchase presliced button mushrooms.

2 tablespoons canola oil, divided
2 medium russet potatoes, peeled and thinly sliced in rounds
1 pound lean ground beef
1 cup minced onions
1 cup sliced button mushrooms
Sea salt
Freshly ground pepper
One 11-ounce can cream of mushroom soup

1. Preheat the oven to 400°F. Coat the interior of an 8-by-8-inch baking dish with 1 tablespoon of oil.

2. Spread out the potatoes in the baking dish. Season with salt and pepper. Bake for 10 minutes.

3. Meanwhile, heat the remaining 1 tablespoon of oil in a skillet over medium-high heat. Cook the ground beef, onions, and mushrooms until the meat is just cooked through, about 5 minutes. Season with salt and pepper. Spread the meat mixture over the parbaked potatoes.

4. Spread the cream of mushroom soup over the meat in the baking dish. Bake uncovered for 15 minutes, or until bubbling.

Cheesy Meatball Casserole

This cheesy casserole is so easy to prepare, and the oven does all the work for you (but check out the tip for a microwave preparation). If you have some time on your hands, prepare the Homemade Meatballs (page 164), and follow all the instructions, except form the meat mixture into 8 meatballs instead of 4. Cook completely before adding to this recipe.

8 dinner rolls, halved horizontally
8 frozen cooked meatballs
16 ounces prepared marinara sauce
4 ounces shredded Italian cheese blend
1 teaspoon canola oil

1 Preheat the oven to 375°F.

2 Separate the dinner rolls into tops and bottoms, and place the bottom halves of the rolls in an 8-by-8-inch casserole dish. Top each roll with 1 meatball.

3 Spread the marinara sauce evenly over this layer, and top with the Italian cheese blend. Finish with the tops to the dinner rolls, and brush with the oil.

4 Cover with foil, and bake for 10 minutes. Remove the foil, and bake for another 5 to 10 minutes, until the cheese is melty and the tops of the rolls are beginning to brown.

- MICROWAVE FRIENDLY
- GOOD FOR SHARING

Serves 4

PREP TIME
5 minutes

COOK TIME
20 minutes

PER SERVING
Calories: 516
Fat: 31g
Carbs: 38g
Fiber: 2g
Protein: 28g

insanely easy
To microwave: Cover the casserole with a microwave-safe lid. Microwave on high for 5 minutes. Remove the lid, and microwave for another 2 to 3 minutes until cooked through.

Seared Steak with Mushrooms in Browned Butter

■ GLUTEN-FREE

Serves 1

PREP TIME
5 minutes

COOK TIME
15 minutes

PER SERVING
(1 STEAK)
Calories: 435
Fat: 26g
Carbs: 3g
Fiber: 0g
Protein: 47g

Dinner for one never tasted so good! I love to make this steak when my vegetarian husband is working late. It works well because steaks are often portioned perfectly for one person. However, if you purchase a larger piece of meat, the meal makes delicious leftovers.

1 tablespoon canola oil
8- to 12-ounce New York strip steak, trimmed of fat
Sea salt
Freshly ground black pepper
2 tablespoons butter
1 cup sliced cremini or button mushrooms
1 teaspoon fresh thyme leaves
1 teaspoon white wine vinegar

1 Heat a large skillet over medium-high heat. Add the oil, and heat for at least 30 seconds.

2 Pat the steak dry with paper towels, and season generously with salt and pepper. Place it in the skillet, and sear for 4 to 5 minutes. Flip the steak, and cook for another 4 to 5 minutes. Set the steak on a cutting board to rest until you're ready to serve.

3 Add the butter to the pan, and cook until it foams. Add the sliced mushrooms, and cook for about 3 minutes to brown. Flip with a pair of tongs, and brown on the other side for 2 minutes. Add the thyme to the pan, and splash with the white wine vinegar to finish. Season the mushrooms with salt and pepper.

4 Serve the steak topped with the mushrooms.

prep tip
Allowing the steak to rest after cooking but before slicing it keeps the juices locked in for a more flavorful piece of meat.

CHOCOLATE BROWNIE MUG CAKE
(PAGE 176)

SWEET TREATS

Peanut Butter Oatmeal Cookies

I grew up making these simple no-bake cookies. They were the answer to my chocolate cravings and so easy to make. Peanut butter works as a binder to hold these goodies together, and the hot cocoa mix adds the chocolate appeal.

Yields 2 dozen cookies

PREP TIME
5 minutes, plus 20 minutes to chill

COOK TIME
2 minutes

PER SERVING (1 COOKIE)
Calories: 111
Fat: 8g
Carbs: 8g
Fiber: 1g
Protein: 4g

¼ cup butter
1 cup peanut butter
1 teaspoon vanilla extract
2 packets hot cocoa mix
1½ cups rolled oats

1 In a small pot, combine the butter, peanut butter, and vanilla extract, and bring to a gentle simmer over medium heat. Cook for 1 minute, and remove the pan from the heat.

2 Stir in the hot cocoa mix and oats until thoroughly mixed.

3 Line a rimmed baking sheet with parchment paper. Scoop the cookie mixture from the pot, and drop 1 tablespoon at a time onto the baking sheet at 1-inch intervals. Refrigerate for 20 minutes to harden. Store the cookies in a covered container.

Classic Sugar Cookies: Beat 1 cup of butter, 1 cup of sugar, and 1 egg until creamy. Add 2 cups of flour, ½ teaspoon of sea salt, and 1 teaspoon of baking soda. Place the dough in 1-inch balls on a cookie sheet, and bake at 350°F for 10 minutes.

Peanut Butter Cookies: Combine 1 cup of peanut butter, 1 cup of brown sugar, 1 egg, ½ cup of flour, and 1 teaspoon of vanilla extract. Form the dough into balls, and press down with a fork. Bake at 325°F for 12 to 15 minutes.

Chocolate Chip Cookies: Beat 1 cup of butter, 1 cup of sugar, and 1 egg until creamy. Add 2 cups of flour, and ½ teaspoon of sea salt. Stir in 1 cup of chocolate chips. Place the dough in 1-inch balls on a cookie sheet, and bake at 350°F for 10 minutes.

prep tip

You can also heat the butter, peanut butter, and vanilla in the microwave for 1 minute. Stir and microwave again for 45 seconds until hot and bubbling.

Chocolate Brownie Mug Cake

■ VEGETARIAN
■ MICROWAVE
  FRIENDLY

Serves 1

PREP TIME
5 minutes

COOK TIME
2 minutes

PER SERVING
(1 MUG CAKE)
Calories: 545
Fat: 36g
Carbs: 56g
Fiber: 4g
Protein: 6g

prep tip
Combine all the
dry ingredients in
individual zip-top
plastic bags so that
they're on hand to
make this mug cake
even easier.

If you're feeling like chocolate cake but don't feel like dirtying a sink full of dishes, try a mug cake. A simple mug serves here as both mixing bowl and cake pan, and a microwave takes the place of the oven. Bonus: The cake is ready in just minutes. If you happen to have powdered sugar on hand, sprinkle or sift 1 teaspoon on top of your mug cake at the end to finish it off.

¼ cup all-purpose flour
2 tablespoons unsweetened cocoa powder
⅛ teaspoon baking soda
Pinch sea salt
3 tablespoons brown sugar
3 tablespoons soft butter
¼ cup hot water

Combine all the ingredients in a microwave-safe mug, and stir to mix. Microwave on high for 1 minute and 45 seconds to 2 minutes, or until the cake is set in the center.

Apple Mug Cake

This mug cake is studded with bits of apple and will remind you of fall. When you're baking with apples, choose Braeburn, Granny Smith, Jonathan, or Gala varieties, which all hold their shape well when cooked. Add a pinch of ground cinnamon and nutmeg for even more autumnal flavors.

¼ cup all-purpose flour
⅛ teaspoon baking soda
½ cup peeled, diced apple
Pinch sea salt
3 tablespoons brown sugar
3 tablespoons soft butter
¼ cup hot water

Combine all the ingredients in a microwave-safe mug, and stir to mix. Microwave on high for 1 minute and 45 seconds to 2 minutes, or until the cake is set in the center.

- VEGETARIAN
- MICROWAVE FRIENDLY

Serves 1

PREP TIME
5 minutes

COOK TIME
2 minutes

PER SERVING (1 MUG CAKE)
Calories: 554
Fat: 35g
Carbs: 59g
Fiber: 2g
Protein: 4g

prep tip
If you don't have a fresh apple, use ½ cup of applesauce, and reduce the hot water to just 3 tablespoons.

Banana Ice Cream

Serves 2

PREP TIME
5 minutes

**PER SERVING
(ABOUT 1 CUP)**
Calories: 210
Fat: 4g
Carbs: 37g
Fiber: 3g
Protein: 9g

prep tip
Freeze bananas on
a baking sheet, then
transfer them to zip-
top plastic bags to
keep the pieces from
sticking together.

Craving ice cream but not keen on all the sugar? Try blended frozen bananas instead. They're naturally sweet and creamy when blended with milk and vanilla. To make it even easier, use vanilla almond milk and skip the vanilla extract.

2 bananas, cut into chunks and frozen
1½ cups 2 percent milk or almond milk
1 teaspoon vanilla extract

Combine all the ingredients in a blender, and purée until smooth.

VARIATIONS

Peppermint Chip Ice Cream: Add ½ teaspoon of mint extract and ½ cup of mini chocolate chips.

Peanut Butter Cup Ice Cream: Crumble 2 peanut butter cups, and stir them into the recipe.

Strawberry Swirl Ice Cream: Add ¼ cup of strawberry jam and 1 cup of frozen strawberries to the recipe.

Blueberry Crumble

Fresh, plump blueberries take center stage in this delicious seasonal dessert. Their natural sweetness reduces the amount of sugar needed in the filling and topping, but the crumble still has all the decadence you're looking for in a dessert. Serve with vanilla ice cream.

5 tablespoons salted butter, cold, divided
4 cups fresh blueberries
½ cup all-purpose flour, plus 1 tablespoon
¼ cup granulated sugar, plus 1 tablespoon
Zest and juice of 1 lemon

1 Preheat the oven to 400°F.

2 Coat the inside of an 8-by-8-inch square baking dish with 1 tablespoon of butter.

3 Add the berries to the baking dish, and sprinkle with 1 tablespoon of flour, 1 tablespoon of sugar, and the lemon juice. Toss gently to mix.

4 In a separate bowl, combine the remaining 4 tablespoons of butter, ½ cup of flour, ¼ cup of sugar, and the lemon zest. Use two butter knives to cut through the butter until the mixture resembles coarse bread crumbs. Sprinkle the mixture over the berries.

5 Bake for 20 to 25 minutes, until the berries are bubbling and the top is beginning to brown. Serve warm or at room temperature.

■ **VEGETARIAN**
■ **GLUTEN-FREE OPTION**
■ **GOOD FOR SHARING**

Serves 4

PREP TIME
10 minutes

COOK TIME
25 minutes

PER SERVING (1 CUP)
Calories: 313
Fat: 15g
Carbs: 45g
Fiber: 4g
Protein: 3g

prep tip
If blueberries aren't in season, use frozen blueberries, but don't defrost them before baking.

substitution tip
To make this gluten-free, substitute a gluten-free flour blend for the all-purpose flour.

Peach Cobbler

- VEGETARIAN
- GLUTEN-FREE OPTION
- GOOD FOR SHARING

Serves 4

PREP TIME
10 minutes

COOK TIME
25 minutes

PER SERVING
(1 CUP)
Calories: 454
Fat: 11g
Carbs: 76g
Fiber: 4g
Protein: 14g

substitution tip
You can use whole-grain or gluten-free pancake mix in this recipe if you want to.

After I learned the basics of baking, using pancake mix was one of the first tricks I learned to improve the texture of homemade desserts. In cookies it produced a dense, chewy texture. In this dessert, it replaces several ingredients and produces a light, fluffy cobbler.

1 tablespoon canola oil
4 peaches, pitted and diced
2 cups pancake mix
1 cup 2 percent milk
2 eggs
4 tablespoons granulated sugar, divided

1 Preheat the oven to 400°F. Coat the inside of an 8-by-8-inch square baking dish with the oil.

2 Add the peaches to the baking dish.

3 In a medium mixing bowl, add the pancake mix, milk, eggs, and 3 tablespoons of sugar. Whisk until no lumps remain. Pour this mixture over the peaches, and tap the baking dish on the counter to allow any air bubbles to escape.

4 Sprinkle the top of the cobbler with the remaining 1 tablespoon of sugar.

5 Bake for 20 to 25 minutes, or until the top is golden brown.

Roasted Pears with Thyme

When I first tried this recipe, I was undone by its simplicity and just how delicious it was. As with any dessert, vanilla ice cream makes it even better. When you slice the pears in half, be sure to leave the stems intact for a pretty presentation.

2 tablespoons butter, at room temperature, divided

4 ripe pears, peeled, halved, and cored

1 tablespoon fresh thyme leaves

2 tablespoons honey

1 pint vanilla ice cream, for serving

1 Preheat the oven to 425°F.

2 Coat the bottom of an 8-by-8-inch baking dish with 1 tablespoon of butter.

3 Place the pears cut-side down in the baking dish, and dot with the remaining 1 tablespoon of butter.

4 Sprinkle the thyme leaves over the pears, and drizzle with the honey.

5 Roast for 25 minutes. Allow to cool for at least 10 minutes before serving. Serve with a scoop of vanilla ice cream.

■ VEGETARIAN
■ GLUTEN-FREE
■ MICROWAVE FRIENDLY
■ GOOD FOR SHARING

Serves 4

PREP TIME
5 minutes

COOK TIME
25 minutes

PER SERVING (1 PEAR AND ½ CUP ICE CREAM)
Calories: 323
Fat: 13g
Carbs: 52g
Fiber: 6g
Protein: 3g

foodie 101
Some tried-and-true fruit-herb pairings include blackberry and rosemary, apple and thyme, dates and sage, and strawberries and basil.

Orange-Chocolate Cake

■ VEGETARIAN
■ GLUTEN-FREE

Serves 4

PREP TIME
5 minutes

COOK TIME
25 minutes

**PER SERVING
(1 PIECE)**
Calories: 535
Fat: 43g
Carbs: 37g
Fiber: 4g
Protein: 6g

prep tip
To grate the orange
zest, run the washed
and dried whole
orange gently over
a fine grater. Stop
when you reach the
white pith; it is bitter.

It doesn't get any easier than this dense orange-chocolate cake. It is so rich and sweet, frosting is redundant. You can also swap the orange for 1 tablespoon of vanilla extract.

½ cup butter, plus 1 tablespoon
3 tablespoons unsweetened cocoa powder, divided
8 ounces dark chocolate chips (60 percent cocoa)
4 eggs
1 orange, zest and 1 tablespoon juice
¼ teaspoon sea salt

1 Preheat the oven to 375°F.

2 Coat the interior of an 8-by-8-inch baking dish with 1 tablespoon of butter. Sprinkle with 1 tablespoon of cocoa powder, and tap the dish gently to thoroughly coat the inside of the pan.

3 Combine the dark chocolate chips and remaining ½ cup of butter in a microwave-safe bowl, and microwave on high for 10 seconds at a time, stirring intermittently, for a total of 1 minute, or until all the chocolate is melted. Allow the chocolate to cool.

4 Place the eggs, orange zest, orange juice, and salt into a blender, and blend on high speed for 1 minute, until nearly doubled in volume.

5 Add the cooled chocolate to the blender, and purée until just combined. Pour the mixture into the prepared baking dish.

6 Bake for 25 minutes, or until set. Sprinkle the remaining cocoa powder over the top of the cake, and allow to cool to room temperature before serving.

Apple Slab Pie with Puff Pastry

Apple pie has always held a soft spot in my heart, but I don't always feel like making pie crust from scratch and rolling it out. Puff pastry is a delicious answer to my dessert dilemma. It is buttery, flaky, and oh so easy.

1 package puff pastry

4 apples, peeled, cored, and very thinly sliced

½ cup brown sugar

1 tablespoon ground cinnamon

2 tablespoons cold butter, cut into small pieces

1. Preheat the oven to 350°F.

2. On a rimmed baking sheet, spread out the puff pastry.

3. Place the apple slices on the puff pastry, and sprinkle evenly with brown sugar and cinnamon. Dot the top of the apples with butter.

4. Bake for 20 minutes, until the apples are soft and the puff pastry is golden.

▦ **VEGETARIAN**

▦ **GOOD FOR SHARING**

Serves 6 to 8

PREP TIME
10 minutes

COOK TIME
20 minutes

PER SERVING (6 SERVINGS)
Calories: 210
Fat: 7g
Carbs: 38g
Fiber: 3g
Protein: 1g

ingredient tip
Use Golden Delicious apples for their sweet flavor and soft texture, or choose Braeburn, Jonathan, Gala, or Granny Smith apples, all juicy and great for baking.

Vegan Chocolate Mousse

- VEGAN
- GLUTEN-FREE
- MICROWAVE FRIENDLY
- PREP AND SERVE

Serves 4

PREP TIME
5 minutes, plus
20 minutes to chill

COOK TIME
2 minutes

PER SERVING
(½ CUP)
Calories: 256
Fat: 14g
Carbs: 29g
Fiber: 3g
Protein: 7g

ingredient tip
Choose chocolate
chips with a high
percentage of cocoa
for the best flavor.
I like 60 percent
cocoa for this recipe.

Most chocolate mousse recipes are made with raw eggs and butter. This vegan version gets its body from tofu. Hey, don't knock it till you've tried it!

1 cup semisweet chocolate chips
1 (8-ounce) package silken tofu
½ cup brewed coffee
1 tablespoon vanilla extract
Pinch sea salt

1 In a microwave-safe bowl, melt the chocolate chips in the microwave on high for 15 seconds. Stir, and cook on high for another 15 seconds. Repeat until the chips are all melted.

2 Scrape the melted chocolate into a blender, and add the tofu, coffee, vanilla, and sea salt. Purée until completely smooth.

3 Divide the mixture between four serving cups, and refrigerate for 20 minutes, until set.

Cookies and Cream Milk Shake

When I was in college, I enjoyed massive cookies and cream milk shakes at a local diner along with platefuls of waffle fries. It was delicious, but it put me on the fast track to gaining the "freshman 15." Now, happily back at my high school weight, I'm eager to indulge in more sensible desserts, such as this one built around creamy frozen bananas and chunks of chocolate sandwich cookies.

1 banana, frozen and cut into chunks
¾ to 1 cup 2 percent milk
1 cup ice cubes
3 chocolate sandwich cookies

1. Combine the banana, ¾ cup of milk, and ice cubes in a blender, and purée until thick and creamy, adding more milk if needed to blend.

2. Add the chocolate sandwich cookies, and blend until only small chunks remain. Serve.

substitution tip: To make this gluten-free, use gluten-free sandwich cookies. To make it vegan, use almond milk and vegan sandwich cookies.

■ VEGETARIAN
■ GLUTEN-FREE OPTION
■ PREP AND SERVE
■ GOOD FOR SHARING

Serves 1

PREP TIME
5 minutes

PER SERVING (1 SHAKE)
Calories: 368
Fat: 11g
Carbs: 61g
Fiber: 4g
Protein: 11g

prep tip
To freeze bananas, cut them into chunks, and spread the chunks out on a plate or baking dish lined with parchment paper. Freeze until solid, and transfer the bananas to a zip-top plastic bag or sealable plastic container.

5-MINUTE GUACAMOLE
(PAGE 188)

KITCHEN STAPLES

5-Minute Guacamole

Yields 1 cup

PREP TIME
5 minutes

PER SERVING
(¼ CUP)
Calories: 165
Fat: 15g
Carbs: 10g
Fiber: 7g
Protein: 2g

leftovers tip
Store leftover guacamole tightly covered in the refrigerator. The lime juice reduces oxidation somewhat, but the top of the guacamole may turn slightly brown. Don't worry, the guacamole underneath is still bright green and flavorful.

Is there anything that fresh guacamole doesn't complement? It's great with everything from corn chips to scrambled eggs. I especially love it on the BRC Bowl (page 120) and Steak Fajitas (page 167).

2 large avocados, peeled and pitted
1 garlic clove, minced
Freshly squeezed juice of 1 lime
1 tablespoon minced cilantro (optional)
¼ cup minced red onion
Sea salt
Freshly ground black pepper

In a medium mixing bowl, combine the avocados, garlic, lime juice, and cilantro (if using). Mash with a fork until the guacamole reaches the desired consistency. Fold in the red onion, and season with salt and pepper.

Hummus

Hummus is a healthy and convenient dip for vegetables or pita bread. It is a good source of complex carbohydrates, healthy fats, and plant-based protein. Serve it with pita bread, carrots, red onions, grape tomatoes, cucumbers, and Kalamata olives for a filling Mediterranean appetizer.

1 (15-ounce) can chickpeas, drained and rinsed
¼ cup tahini
1 garlic clove
Freshly squeezed juice of 1 lemon
2 tablespoons extra-virgin olive oil
¼ teaspoon sea salt

In a blender jar, combine the chickpeas, tahini, garlic, lemon juice, olive oil, and salt. Purée until smooth.

VARIATION

Roasted Red Pepper Hummus: Add 1 cup of roughly chopped roasted red peppers to the hummus recipe, and blend until smooth.

▪ VEGAN
▪ GLUTEN-FREE
▪ PREP AND SERVE

Serves 4

PREP TIME
5 minutes

**PER SERVING
(¼ CUP)**
Calories: 237
Fat: 16g
Carbs: 19g
Fiber: 6g
Protein: 7g

foodie 101
Tahini is ground hulled sesame seeds. It is used in Mediterranean and Middle Eastern cooking. It is sold in both shelf-stable and refrigerated versions but should be refrigerated once the container is opened.

Fresh Salsa

■ VEGAN
■ GLUTEN-FREE
■ PREP AND SERVE
■ GOOD FOR
  SHARING

Yields 2 cups

PREP TIME
10 minutes

PER SERVING
(½ CUP)
Calories: 29
Fat: 0g
Carbs: 6g
Fiber: 2g
Protein: 1g

prep tip
Jalapeño peppers
have a moderate
level of heat, but
if they're too spicy
for your taste, care-
fully slice away the
membranes and
seeds before minc-
ing and adding it to
the salsa.

When I was in college, my parents purchased a salsa maker from an infomercial. It was similar to a hand-crank food processor. Eventually, we sold it at a garage sale and opted for the only tool you really need to make fresh salsa: a sharp knife. Chop up a few essential ingredients, and you have restaurant-worthy salsa ready in minutes!

1 pound ripe tomatoes, cored and diced
1 small red onion, minced
1 jalapeño pepper, minced
¼ cup minced cilantro
1 tablespoon freshly squeezed lime juice
Sea salt
Freshly ground black pepper

In a nonreactive bowl, mix the tomatoes, onion, jalapeño, cilantro, and lime juice. Season with salt and pepper. Enjoy immediately, or store the leftovers in a covered container in the refrigerator.

Homemade Trail Mix

When you make your own trail mix, you get to decide which nuts and fruits to use according to your taste and budget. Sunflower seeds and peanuts are the least expensive options, almonds and walnuts are priced in the middle, and shelled pistachios, hazelnuts, and macadamia nuts are the most expensive. Buy in bulk from the health food section of the grocery store for the best prices and selection.

1 cup roasted almonds
1 cup salted peanuts
1 cup dried cranberries
1 cup chocolate chips

Combine all the ingredients, and store in a covered container.

VARIATIONS

Monkey Business Trail Mix: Mix 1 cup peanuts, 1 cup almonds, 1 cup dried bananas, and 1 cup chocolate chips.

Cherry Pie Trail Mix: Mix 1 cup pecans, 1 cup almonds, 1 cup dried cherries, and 1 cup white chocolate chips.

Fall Flavors Trail Mix: Mix 1 cup walnuts, 1 cup pepitas, 1 cup sliced dried apricots, and 1 cup dried cranberries.

▪ VEGAN
▪ GLUTEN-FREE
▪ PREP AND SERVE
▪ GOOD FOR SHARING

Yields 4 cups

PREP TIME
5 minutes

**PER SERVING
(½ CUP)**
Calories: 402
Fat: 25g
Carbs: 44g
Fiber: 7g
Protein: 10g

leftovers tip
Store trail mix in a cool place away from direct sunlight to avoid melting the chocolate.

Sweet and Spicy Snack Mix

- VEGAN
- MICROWAVE FRIENDLY
- GOOD FOR SHARING

This snack mix is so much better than the bagged stuff in the snack aisle of the grocery store. Just pop it in the oven, and your room- or dorm mates will all emerge and wander to the kitchen for a taste.

Yields 7 cups

PREP TIME
5 minutes

COOK TIME
20 to 25 minutes

PER SERVING (½ CUP)
Calories: 256
Fat: 18g
Carbs: 21g
Fiber: 2g
Protein: 4g

prep tip
To make in the microwave, combine the cereal, nuts, and pretzels in a microwave-safe bowl. Whisk the hot sauce, sugar, oil, and salt in another bowl, and pour it over the cereal mix. Microwave on high 5 minutes, stirring every 2 minutes.

4 cups Rice Chex or Corn Chex cereal

2 cups mixed nuts

1 cup pretzel sticks

1 tablespoon hot sauce

¼ cup brown sugar

½ cup canola oil

½ teaspoon sea salt

1 Preheat the oven to 350°F.

2 In a large mixing bowl, add the Chex cereal, nuts, and pretzel sticks, and stir to combine.

3 In a small bowl, whisk together the hot sauce, sugar, oil, and salt, and pour it over the cereal mix.

4 Spread out the mixture on a rimmed baking sheet. Bake for 10 minutes. Stir, and bake for another 10 to 15 minutes, or until the cereal and nuts are beginning to crisp. They will continue to get crunchier once they're out of the oven.

5 Allow to rest for 5 minutes before serving, and allow to cool completely before storing in a covered container.

Balsamic Vinaigrette

This sweet and tangy salad dressing complements green salads and pairs well with fruits such as pomegranates, dried cranberries, and pears. It also makes an excellent marinade for chicken.

3 tablespoons balsamic vinegar
1 teaspoon honey
1 teaspoon minced fresh basil
1 shallot, minced
¼ cup extra-virgin olive oil
Sea salt
Freshly ground black pepper

In a small mixing bowl, combine the balsamic vinegar, honey, basil, and shallot. Slowly drizzle in the olive oil, whisking constantly to emulsify. Season with salt and pepper.

■ VEGETARIAN
■ GLUTEN-FREE
■ PREP AND SERVE

Yields ½ cup

PREP TIME
5 minutes

PER SERVING
(2 TABLESPOONS)
Calories: 138
Fat: 14g
Carbs: 4g
Fiber: 0g
Protein: 0g

prep tip
You can also make this dressing in a glass jar with a lid: Add the ingredients, tighten the lid, and shake to emulsify the oil.

Creamy Caesar Dressing

Yields ½ cup

PREP TIME
5 minutes

PER SERVING
(2 TABLESPOONS)
Calories: 218
Fat: 24g
Carbs: 1g
Fiber: 0g
Protein: 1g

Minced anchovies are commonly used ingredients in this classic salad dressing, but it was a surprise to find whole anchovies staring up at me from my Caesar salad when I ordered it in Europe. In this version, the anchovy paste is optional. The recipe also uses mayonnaise and Dijon mustard for thickening, instead of raw egg yolks.

3 tablespoons freshly squeezed lemon juice
1 teaspoon Dijon mustard
3 garlic cloves, minced
1 teaspoon anchovy paste (optional)
2 tablespoons mayonnaise
⅓ cup canola oil
Sea salt
Freshly ground black pepper

In a small mixing bowl, combine the lemon juice, mustard, garlic, anchovy paste (if using), and mayonnaise. Slowly drizzle in the oil, whisking constantly to emulsify. Season with salt and pepper.

Sesame-Ginger Dressing

Sour lime juice, sweet honey, spicy ginger, and complex toasted sesame oil are an addicting combination in this simple Asian salad dressing. Use it to dip salad rolls, drizzle over rice noodles, or enjoy with the Sesame-Ginger Chopped Salad (page 78).

3 tablespoons freshly squeezed lime juice

1 teaspoon honey

1 teaspoon minced ginger

1 teaspoon minced garlic

1 tablespoon toasted sesame oil

¼ cup canola oil

Sea salt

Freshly ground black pepper

In a small mixing bowl, combine the lime juice, honey, ginger, garlic, and sesame oil. Slowly drizzle in the oil, whisking constantly to emulsify. Season with salt and pepper.

▪ **VEGETARIAN**
▪ **GLUTEN-FREE**
▪ **PREP AND SERVE**

Yields ½ cup

PREP TIME
5 minutes

**PER SERVING
(2 TABLESPOONS)**
Calories: 160
Fat: 17g
Carbs: 3g
Fiber: 0g
Protein: 0g

substitution tip
To make this salad dressing vegan, use 1 teaspoon of maple syrup or ¾ teaspoon of agave nectar in place of the honey.

Glossary

AL DENTE: Food that is slightly chewy when bitten, particularly when referring to pasta, which should be cooked "to the tooth."

BASTE: To pour cooking juices or other melted fats over a food to keep it moist while cooking.

BLANCH AND SHOCK: To cook food briefly in boiling water and then plunge it into ice water to stop the cooking process. This technique preserves color and texture, especially when used for cooking vegetables.

BRAISE: To cook food that is partially submerged in liquid.

FOLD: To incorporate one ingredient into the other without introducing too much air or deflating something that is already airy and light, such as egg whites or whipped cream.

MINCE: To cut food into very small pieces that will not be discernible in the finished food. The technique is most commonly used in the preparation of ginger and garlic.

MIREPOIX: Equal parts diced onion, carrots, and celery. This mixture can be prepared, or purchased in the grocery store. Look for it near other refrigerated produce.

POACH: To cook food that is completely submerged in liquid.

SAUTÉ: To cook over high heat in oil. This technique is useful for preparing vegetables to cook them without causing them to soften too much.

SCORE: To make several shallow cuts across the surface of a piece of meat, a fruit, or a vegetable. With meat, the technique is used to help absorb marinade. With fruits, scoring is often used to remove skin after blanching.

SEAR: A technique used in grilling, braising, and roasting of a food until a deep caramelization occurs on its surface.

SEASON: To add salt and pepper to a food to give it the desirable balance with other flavors in the dish.

ZEST: The brightly colored outer-skin layer of a citrus fruit. A paring knife, vegetable peeler, box grater, Microplane, or citrus zester is needed to remove the zest from the fruit.

References

Johnson, Elizabeth, Rohini Vishwanathan, Emily Mohn, Jordan Haddock, Helen Rasmussen, and Tammy Scott. "Avocado Consumption Increases Neural Lutein and Improves Cognitive Function." *The FASEB Journal* 29, no. 1, S32.8 (April 2015). Accessed September 19, 2016. www.fasebj.org/content /29/1_Supplement/32.8.short.

Sorgen, Carol. "Eat Smart for a Healthier Brain." WebMD. December 18, 2008. Accessed September 19, 2016. www.webmd.com/diet/features /eat-smart-healthier-brain#1.

Zeisel, S. H. "Nutritional Importance of Choline for Brain Development." *Journal of the American College of Nutrition* 23, no. S6 (2004): 621S–626S. Accessed September 19, 2016. www.ncbi.nlm.nih.gov/pubmed/15640516.

The Dirty Dozen and the Clean Fifteen

A nonprofit environmental watchdog organization called Environmental Working Group (EWG) looks at data supplied by the U.S. Department of Agriculture (USDA) and the Food and Drug Administration (FDA) about pesticide residues. Each year it compiles a list of the best and worst pesticide loads found in commercial crops. You can use these lists to decide which fruits and vegetables to buy organic to minimize your exposure to pesticides and which produce is considered safe enough to buy conventionally. This does not mean they are pesticide-free, though, so wash these fruits and vegetables thoroughly.

These lists change every year, so make sure you look up the most recent one before you fill your shopping cart. The produce listed below is from the 2016 list. You'll find the most recent lists as well as a guide to pesticides in produce at EWG.org/FoodNews.

Dirty Dozen

Apples
Celery
Cherries
Cherry tomatoes
Cucumbers
Grapes
Nectarines
Peaches
Spinach
Strawberries
Sweet bell peppers
Tomatoes

In addition to the Dirty Dozen, the EWG added two types of produce contaminated with highly toxic organo-phosphate insecticides:

Kale/collard greens
Hot peppers

Clean Fifteen

Asparagus
Avocados
Cabbage
Cantaloupes (domestic)
Cauliflower
Eggplants
Grapefruits
Honeydew melons
Kiwis
Mangos
Onions

Papayas
Pineapples
Sweet corn
Sweet peas (frozen)

Measurement Conversions

Volume Equivalents (Liquid)

U.S. STANDARD	U.S. STANDARD (OUNCES)	METRIC (APPROXIMATE)
2 tablespoons	1 fl. oz.	30 mL
¼ cup	2 fl. oz.	60 mL
½ cup	4 fl. oz.	120 mL
1 cup	8 fl. oz.	240 mL
1½ cups	12 fl. oz.	355 mL
2 cups or 1 pint	16 fl. oz.	475 mL
4 cups or 1 quart	32 fl. oz.	1 L
1 gallon	128 fl. oz.	4 L

Oven Temperatures

FAHRENHEIT	CELSIUS (APPROXIMATE)
250°F	120°C
300°F	150°C
325°F	165°C
350°F	180°C
375°F	190°C
400°F	200°C
425°F	220°C
450°F	230°C

Weight Equivalents

U.S. STANDARD	METRIC (APPROXIMATE)
½ ounce	15 g
1 ounce	30 g
2 ounces	60 g
4 ounces	115 g
8 ounces	225 g
12 ounces	340 g
16 ounces or 1 pound	455 g

Volume Equivalents (Dry)

U.S. STANDARD	METRIC (APPROXIMATE)
⅛ teaspoon	0.5 mL
¼ teaspoon	1 mL
½ teaspoon	2 mL
¾ teaspoon	4 mL
1 teaspoon	5 mL
1 tablespoon	15 mL
¼ cup	59 mL
⅓ cup	79 mL
½ cup	118 mL
⅔ cup	156 mL
¾ cup	177 mL
1 cup	235 mL
2 cups or 1 pint	475 mL
3 cups	700 mL
4 cups or 1 quart	1 L

Recipe Index

	GLUTEN-FREE or GF option	VEGAN or Vegan option	VEGETARIAN or Vegetarian option	MICROWAVE FRIENDLY	PREP AND SERVE	GOOD FOR SHARING
5-Minute Guacamole, 188	X	X	X		X	X
Apple Mug Cake, 177			X	X		
Apple Slab Pie with Puff Pastry, 183			X			X
Asian Kale Salad, 77	X	X	X		X	X
Avocado-Bacon Toast, 59						
Avocado-Chicken Open-Face Sandwich, 59						
Avocado Toast with Poached Egg and Tomato Salad, 59			X			
Bacon-Wrapped Dates, 69	X					X
Baked French Toast, 55			X			X
Baked Veggie Quesadilla, 91			X	X		X
Balsamic Vinaigrette, 193	X		X		X	
Banana Ice Cream, 178	X	X	X		X	X
Banana Mocha Protein Shake, 42	X		X		X	
Basic Burger, 92–93						X
Basic Scrambled Eggs, 46	X		X			
Blueberry Crumble, 179	X		X			X
Blueberry Power Greens Smoothie, 38	X	X			X	X
BRC Bowl, 120	X	X	X	X		

	GLUTEN-FREE or GF option	VEGAN or Vegan option	VEGETARIAN or Vegetarian option	MICROWAVE FRIENDLY	PREP AND SERVE	GOOD FOR SHARING
Broccoli-Cheddar Quiche, 127			X			
Broccoli-Cheddar Soup, 106	X		X			
Brown Sugar–Glazed Ham, 163	X					X
Bruschetta, 70		X	X			X
Caprese Salad, 81	X		X		X	
Cheesy Meatball Casserole, 169				X		X
Cheesy Stuffed Chicken in Salsa Verde, 145						
Cherry-Pecan Oatmeal, 45	X		X	X		
Cherry Pie Trail Mix, 191	X		X		X	X
Chicken Provençal, 147	X					
Chicken Salad Wrap, 89					X	
Chicken, Sausage, and White Bean Cassoulet, 157	X					
Chicken Soup, 100	X					X
Chicken with Mushrooms and Onions, 145	X					
Chimichurri Beef, 166	X					X
Chipotle Black Bean Chili, 103	X	X	X			
Chocolate Brownie Mug Cake, 176			X	X		
Chocolate Chip Cookies, 175			X			X
Chorizo and Kidney Bean Chili, 102	X					X
Cinnamon-Raisin Oatmeal, 44	X		X	X		

	GLUTEN-FREE or GF option	VEGAN or Vegan option	VEGETARIAN or Vegetarian option	MICROWAVE FRIENDLY	PREP AND SERVE	GOOD FOR SHARING
Classic French Toast, 54			X			X
Classic Grilled Cheese, 82			X			
Classic Sugar Cookies, 175			X			X
Cookies and Cream Milk Shake, 185	X		X		X	X
Coriander-Crusted Chicken Breasts, 148–149	X					
Corn Chowder, 108	X	X	X			
Crab and Artichoke Linguine, 141						X
Creamy Avocado Toast, 58		X	X			
Creamy Caesar Dressing, 194	X		X		X	
Creamy Chicken and Mushroom Fettuccini, 150–151						
Creamy Kale and Banana Smoothie, 38	X	X	X		X	X
Creamy Salsa Verde Taquitos, 68	X	X	X			X
Curried Lentil Soup, 107	X	X	X			X
Eggplant, Bell Pepper, and Pineapple Curry, 132	X	X	X			
Essential Tuna Salad Sandwich, 87					X	
Everyday Kale Salad, 76	X	X	X		X	X
Fall Flavors Trail Mix, 191	X	X	X		X	X
Fresh Salsa, 190	X	X	X		X	X
Fried Rice, 160	X					X
Garlicky Cauliflower Linguini, 116	X	X	X			

	GLUTEN-FREE or GF option	VEGAN or Vegan option	VEGETARIAN or Vegetarian option	MICROWAVE FRIENDLY	PREP AND SERVE	GOOD FOR SHARING
Gazpacho, 104	X	X	X		X	
Go-To Green Smoothie, 38	X	X	X		X	X
Granola, 52	X		X			X
Greek Pita Sandwich, 86			X		X	
Green Bean and Apple Salad with Almonds, 84	X	X	X	X		
Green Mango Lassi Smoothie, 38	X	X	X		X	X
Ham and Cheese Breakfast Sandwich, 53	X					
Ham-Stuffed Chicken Breast, 144						
Hard-Boiled Eggs, 49	X		X			
Havarti-Mushroom Pizza, 119			X	X		
Hoisin-Ginger Tofu Stir-Fry, 131	X	X	X			
Homemade Meatballs, 164						X
Homemade Trail Mix, 191	X	X	X		X	X
Honey-Soy Salmon, 138	X			X		
Honey-Yogurt Fruit Dip, 65	X		X		X	
Hummus, 189	X	X	X		X	
Italian Sausage, Pepper, and Onion Skillet, 161	X					
Kale Caesar Salad, 77	X		X		X	X
Kale, Pear, and Pecan Salad, 77	X	X	X		X	X
Kung Pao Chickpeas, 62		X	X	X		X

	GLUTEN-FREE or GF option	VEGAN or Vegan option	VEGETARIAN or Vegetarian option	MICROWAVE FRIENDLY	PREP AND SERVE	GOOD FOR SHARING
Lemon Chicken, 146	X					
Loaded Sweet Potatoes, 125	X	X	X			
Macaroni and Cheese, 114			X			
Mason Jar Chia Pudding, 43	X	X	X		X	
Meatloaf, 165						
Miso Ramen, 97		X	X	X		X
Monkey Business Trail Mix, 191	X		X		X	X
Mozzarella Sticks, 71			X	X		X
Mushroom Barley Soup, 109		X	X			X
No-Bake Energy Balls, 63	X	X	X	X	X	X
Omelet, 48	X		X			
Orange-Chocolate Cake, 182	X		X			
Pan-Seared Chicken with Zucchini, 145	X					
Pasta Puttanesca, 115		X	X			X
Peach Cobbler, 180	X		X			X
Peanut Butter–Banana French Toast, 55			X			X
Peanut Butter Cookies, 175			X	X		X
Peanut Butter Cup Ice Cream, 178	X		X		X	X
Peanut Butter Cup Smoothie, 40	X	X	X		X	X
Peanut Butter Oatmeal Cookies, 174			X	X		X

	GLUTEN-FREE or GF option	VEGAN or Vegan option	VEGETARIAN or Vegetarian option	MICROWAVE FRIENDLY	PREP AND SERVE	GOOD FOR SHARING
Peanut Butter Yogurt Spread, 66	X		X		X	X
Peppermint Chip Ice Cream, 178	X		X		X	X
Pizza Margherita, 119			X	X		
Pizza Margherita Grilled Cheese, 83			X			
Poached Eggs, 49	X		X			
Pork Chops with Onions and Apples, 162	X					
Potato, Beef, and Mushroom Casserole, 168						X
Potato-Onion Frittata, 50	X		X			
Prosciutto, Provolone, and Pear Grilled Cheese, 83						
Pumpkin Spice Shake, 41	X		X		X	
Quinoa Taco Casserole, 121	X		X			
Ramen, 96		X	X	X		X
Ramen with Soft-Boiled Egg, 97			X	X		X
Raspberry-Almond French Toast, 55			X			X
Roasted Pears with Thyme, 181	X		X	X		X
Roasted Red Pepper and Provolone Sandwich, 88			X		X	
Roasted Red Pepper and Tomato Soup, 98–99	X	X	X			
Roasted Red Pepper Hummus, 189	X	X	X		X	
Roasted Root Vegetable Frittata, 126	X		X			
Roasted Spaghetti Squash, 113	X	X	X			X

	GLUTEN-FREE or GF option	VEGAN or Vegan option	VEGETARIAN or Vegetarian option	MICROWAVE FRIENDLY	PREP AND SERVE	GOOD FOR SHARING
Roasted Squash with Lemon-Garlic Yogurt, 61	X		X			
Roasted-Vegetable Chilaquiles, 122–123	X		X	X		
Roasted Vegetables with Orzo and Feta, 117	X		X			
Salmon Sliders with Avocado, 85					X	
Seared Steak with Mushrooms in Browned Butter, 170–171	X					
Sesame-Ginger Chopped Salad, 78	X	X	X		X	X
Sesame-Ginger Dressing, 195	X		X		X	
Shakshuka, 130	X		X			
Shredded-Chicken Street Tacos, 152–153	X					
Shrimp Cocktail, 137	X					X
Shrimp Fajitas, 137						X
Shrimp Scampi, 136						X
Skillet Shepherd's Pie, 165	X					X
Soba Noodle & Veggie Stir-Fry, 133			X			
Soft-Boiled Eggs, 49	X		X			
Southwestern Skillet, 51	X		X			
Spaghetti Marinara, 112–113		X				X
Spaghetti with Mushrooms and Herbs, 113			X			X
Spicy Bacon Grilled Cheese, 83						

	GLUTEN-FREE or GF option	VEGAN or Vegan option	VEGETARIAN or Vegetarian option	MICROWAVE FRIENDLY	PREP AND SERVE	GOOD FOR SHARING
Spicy Shrimp and Soba Noodles, 140	X					X
Spinach and Artichoke Dip, 67	X		X	X		X
Spring Mix Salad with Quinoa and Dried Cranberries, 79	X	X	X			X
Steak Fajitas, 167	X					X
Strawberry Swirl Ice Cream, 178	X	X	X		X	X
Stuffed Mushrooms, 73			X			X
Super Cheesy Lasagna, 118			X	X		
Sweet and Spicy Snack Mix, 192		X	X	X		X
Sweet Potato Fries with Chipotle Mayo, 60	X		X			X
Tacos, 165						X
Teriyaki Chicken Bowl, 154–155						X
Thai Chicken Ramen, 97				X		X
Thai Ginger Chicken, 156	X					
Thai Lettuce Cups, 72	X					X
Thai Peanut Noodles, 128–129	X	X	X			
Thai Peanut Sauce, 129			X		X	
Tomato-Basil Braised Cod, 139	X			X		
Tomato-Basil Soup, 99	X	X	X			X
Tortellini Soup, 101			X			
Tortilla Soup, 105	X					X

	GLUTEN-FREE or GF option	VEGAN or Vegan option	VEGETARIAN or Vegetarian option	MICROWAVE FRIENDLY	PREP AND SERVE	GOOD FOR SHARING
Tropical Breakfast Smoothie, 39	X	X	X		X	
Tuna Cakes with Potato Skins, 142–143	X					
Tuna Melt, 87						
Tuna-Stuffed Avocado, 87	X				X	
Vegan Chocolate Mousse, 184	X	X	X	X	X	
Vegan Enchiladas, 124		X	X	X		
Vegetable Wrap with Hummus, 90		X	X		X	
Vegetarian Greek Pita Sandwich, 86			X			
Watermelon, Tomato, and Feta Salad, 80	X		X		X	X
Yogurt Bark, 64		X	X			X
Zucchini Noodle Spaghetti, 113	X		X			X

Index

About the Author

PAMELA ELLGEN is a food blogger, certified personal trainer, and author of several books on cooking, nutrition, and fitness, including *The Healthy Slow Cooker Cookbook* and *The Gluten-Free Cookbook for Families*. In addition to maintaining her own food blog at PamelasModernFamilyTable.com, her work has been published by *The Huffington Post*, *The Daily Meal*, LIVESTRONG, *Darling Magazine*, and Spinning.com. A proud graduate of Washington State University, Pamela now lives in California with her husband and two sons.

CPSIA information can be obtained
at www.ICGtesting.com
Printed in the USA
LVHW022038080919
630310LV00001B/1/P

9 781623 158576